Dear Grace

Dear Grace

Answers to Questions about the Faith

Grace D. MacKinnon

Our Sunday Visitor Publishing Division
Our Sunday Visitor, Inc.
Huntington, Indiana 46750

Nihil Obstat
Rev. Brian Van Hove, S.J., S.T.L., Ph.D.
Censor Deputatus

Imprimatur
Most Rev. Raymundo J. Peña, D.D.
Bishop of Brownsville
August 19, 2002

The *Nihil Obstat* and *Imprimatur* are official declarations that a book or pamphlet is free from doctrinal or moral error. It is not implied that those who have granted the *Nihil Obstat* and *Imprimatur* agree with the contents, opinions, or statements expressed.

This work is based on the author's column, "Dear Grace," and has received some minor revisions for stylistic consistency and other editorial considerations and, most important of all, the inclusion of the latest revisions of Church documents, including, for instance, the *General Instruction of the Roman Missal* (2000 edition).

Scripture citations used in this work are taken from the *Catholic Edition of the Revised Standard Version of the Bible* (RSV), copyright © 1965 and 1966 by the Division of Christian Education of the National Council of the Churches of Christ in the United States of America. Used by permission. All rights reserved.

Excerpts from the English translation of the *Catechism of the Catholic Church*, second edition, for use in the United States of America, copyright © 1994 and 1997, United States Catholic Conference—Libreria Editrice Vaticana. Used by permission. All rights reserved.

Excerpts from the Code of Canon Law and from various Vatican documents — among them papal encyclicals, apostolic exhortations, and the like — are gleaned from a number of sources, including those found on the Internet.

Every reasonable effort has been made to determine copyright holders of excerpted materials and to secure permissions as needed. If any copyrighted materials have been inadvertently used in this work without proper credit being given in one form or another, please notify Our Sunday Visitor in writing so that future printings of this work may be corrected accordingly.

Our Sunday Visitor Publishing Division
Our Sunday Visitor, Inc.
200 Noll Plaza
Huntington, IN 46750

ISBN: 1-931709-80-7 (Inventory No. T45)
LCCN: 2002115707

Cover design by Monica Haneline
Cover photo copyright © 1998 EyeWire, Inc.
Interior design by Sherri L. Hoffman

PRINTED IN THE UNITED STATES OF AMERICA

To my mother,
Consuelo T. McClain:
One of the greatest "moments of grace" of my life.

Table of Contents

Preface

God always surprises us by those whom He chooses to help build up His Kingdom. Most of the great apparitions, for example, were granted to poor, small people — those who looked weak in the eyes of the world — but whose hearts, however, were pure and in search of God. Let us think of Juan Diego at Guadalupe, Bernadette at Lourdes, Lucia de Jesús and her cousins Francisco and Jacinta Marto at Fátima. None of them would have been the choice of the "wise" men of this world. But they were God's choice because His ways are not our ways, and He achieves His purpose best by reminding us that He is the one who achieves victory while using seemingly weak human instruments whose strength is to recognize their weakness while putting all their trust in God. For it is in their "weakness" that God reveals His power and His message all the more.

One of these whom He chose was Grace — and it is providential indeed that her name is Grace, because the work she has accomplished and still accomplishes cannot be explained except by and through God's grace.

Here is a woman who, from her very birth, made the acquaintance of the Cross. Born with a physical disability, she had to fight against the greatest odds in her constant struggles from day to day. Carried by "grace," however, she understood that the Cross is the way to supernatural victory. Grace conquered discouragement, and realized that — difficult as her life was — she could overcome defeat. She decided to learn her faith, and because she was faithful, she learned it well. But she also learned that faith is not something to be accepted only intellectually, but that it must be lived.

Having completed her degree in theology, Grace waited for God to call her. She understood that she was to share the knowledge she had obtained with "blood, sweat, and tears." By dint of constant effort and sacrifice, she began to write weekly columns in a local newspaper and invited readers to submit their questions and difficulties. In her heart was a profound longing to teach the truths of the Catholic faith, and she was especially sensitive to the needs of those to whom it had not been properly taught. God had prepared her for this and He visibly blessed her work. With time, many people learned of her writing and its clear explanation of Catholic doctrine. With and through the Cross, God was giving her the immense consolation of sharing her knowledge and love of truth with others. And she does so to this day.

Dear Grace offers the hungry souls of the faithful an amazing array of topics: from the dogmatic to the moral, from the moral to the liturgical, from the liturgical to the timely and urgent. Grace addresses herself to a large audience, and her unique and great gift is that she answers their questions with empathy, love, and understanding, while at the same time remaining firmly grounded in the teachings of the Church. Her columns are well documented with quotations from Holy Scripture, from the *Catechism of the Catholic Church*, and the writings of the popes.

Grace now has a huge mission and helps thousands of starving souls — people hungry to learn the truths of their faith. We should realize that what she is accomplishing is the work of God — the work of grace. And this grace has made her faithful in spite of the daily hurdles that she even now still encounters along her path.

Grace has changed defeat into a victory for God. Thank you, Dear Grace!

Alice von Hildebrand, Ph.D.

Introduction

Little did I know back in 1992, as I began theological studies, that God was about to unfold a very special plan for my life. How could I possibly have known then that one day I would be writing a newspaper column on the Catholic faith? He is indeed a God of surprises. The idea for the "Dear Grace" column was born from a profoundly strong and deeply felt sense of mission. Although I had been Catholic all my life, many of those years were spent not knowing or understanding the faith very well. At one point, I asked, "How can one possibly live it if he or she does not fully grasp it?" I was certain there were many others like me out there. It was the beginning of a journey, one that continues to this day.

Since 1997, hundreds of people have attended the courses I have offered. One of the most popular has been the basic fundamental series titled *Come Fall in Love With Jesus Christ*. This instruction in the basic teachings of the Catholic faith is what we so desperately need. It has been amazing to see the response — the hunger that Catholics have for increasing their knowledge of God and His ways. I have witnessed lives being changed, and it has truly been a blessing and privilege to be part of it all.

Always, wherever I have taught, there have been an unending number of questions, so many questions! Every one of them deserves to be answered. But how would we do this? One day, as we sat and talked about it, my sister Rosalie asked, "Why don't you write a column in the newspaper?" That sounded like a great idea! If only we could utilize the secular media to reach people and help them learn about God!

Never will I forget the day I telephoned George Cox — the editor, at that time, of the *Brownsville Herald* — to inquire about the possibility of running a weekly column answering questions about the Catholic faith. After pointing out to him that the Lower Rio Grande Valley of south Texas is (in percentages) the most Catholic area in the entire United States, he agreed to do it! And it was only the beginning. A few months later, the Harlingen *Valley Morning Star* began publishing it as well. Many other newspapers, both Catholic and secular, have since then begun to carry the column in their papers, and it is now published as far away as Ireland, Korea, and Japan.

This book is a collection of the first two years of "Dear Grace," which made its debut in August of 1999. I wish to make it available owing to the numerous requests I have received for copies of the column. Many people have shared that they clip them out each week but sometimes have missed some.

I would like to thank the Bishop of the Diocese of Brownsville, the Most Reverend Raymundo J. Peña, for his continued support in this mission and for allowing me to assist him in teaching the Catholic faith to the people under his care.

There have been so many others who have helped me along the way, too many to list! First, I must thank my daughter Crystal Ann and my seven sisters — Rosalie, Velma, Janie, Susan, Diana, Perla, and Sandy — all have been a constant source of support and love. Where would one be without one's family? Our beautiful mother, Consuelo McClain, passed away in 1997, but she left her mark on our lives forever. Hers was a pure and giving heart, one that was always ready to sacrifice for her children. She was an example to us all of the love that God has for every human soul.

The road toward obtaining a graduate degree in theology was not an easy one, but on that road God sent me wonderful people who encouraged and inspired me. Among them were Monsignor Paul Procella, Father Philip A. Wilhite, Father John J. Corapi, Monsignor James B. Anderson, Father Stephen P. Zigrang, and Father Steven Nesrsta. Thank you especially, Monsignor Anderson, for being such a holy man of God and a great professor of theology. From you I learned so many of the beautiful truths of the Catholic faith. Every time I sat in your class, I fell more in love with God.

A special thank-you also goes to Father Brian Van Hove, S.J., the current *Censor Deputatus* for the Diocese of Brownsville, and former *Censor Deputatus* Father Carlos Zuniga, who have read my column each week before publication. Father Van Hove deserves an extra note of thanks for the patient assistance he gave in reviewing the manuscript and for help with some of the preliminary editing. Thank you, Father Brian! I could not have done it without you!

In addition, I wish to thank Charlie and Carol Vaughan, and Sam and Margaret Pate, for the tremendous support they have given me — especially to Charlie, who declared the day he met me, "Grace, you are 'a well-kept secret.' Many people do not yet know about you, but that's going to change." His enthusiasm as well as his assistance is sincerely appreciated.

I must also express gratitude to my students. On so many nights when I had to drive far from my home — sometimes on dark country roads — it was your eager, happy, and welcoming faces that made it all worthwhile. How I wish you knew what an honor it has been to be your teacher. And I have learned the faith more and more, right along with you. You showed up on many evenings when you could have easily chosen to do something else. May God bless you abundantly for answering His call to come to know Him.

My friends all know who they are and how much I love them and how grateful I am to them. And, of course, my readers! It is because of you that "Dear Grace" has continued and grown. Thank you for your sincere and interesting questions and for giving me the opportunity to serve you. Keep writing. I love hearing from you!

Grace D. MacKinnon
Brownsville, Texas

(Grace MacKinnon may be reached by e-mail at grace@DearGrace.com or via the Internet at www.DearGrace.com. Her teaching audiotapes and CDs are available through St. Joseph Communications at www.saintjoe.com or call 1-800-526-2151.)

1
Church Doctrine

Dear Grace,

Why do Catholics pray to the saints, when the Bible tells us that Jesus is the only mediator between God and man?

This is a question that is often asked of Catholics. The teaching of the Church is clear: Jesus Christ is the only mediator between God and man. No other person in heaven or on earth can take His place. The role of Mary or any other saint is to lead the person to Christ. When the saints pray for us, they receive their power from Christ Himself. They do not possess this power on their own.

This intercessory prayer of the saints is a powerful way that Catholics show their belief in the beautiful doctrine of the communion of saints, which states that the saints in heaven, the souls in purgatory, and the faithful on earth are involved and concerned with one another's eternal salvation. In other words, the Catholic Church believes that her members, the saints, exist not only on earth, but in purgatory and heaven as well. Intercessory prayer declares our love for one another in the Church as well as our faith that our ties to Christ and His Church forged in Baptism cannot be broken by death (see *Catechism of the Catholic Church* [CCC], n. 1267ff).

If we can ask a fellow Christian, who is living and still struggling in this life, to pray for us, then why can we not ask a saint whom the Church affirms to be in heaven to pray for us? What a wonderful feeling and consolation it is to know that there is someone in heaven praying for us.

Dear Grace,

Why do Catholics believe in the resurrection of the body after death? When does this actually happen?

The Bible tells us that when Jesus returns to earth, He will physically raise all those who have died, giving them bodies they seem to have lost at the end of their earthly life. These will be the same bodies they had while they lived on earth. Did not Jesus have the same body after He rose from the dead? Yet, it was different. His followers were unable to recognize Him at first, but later they did. Because He had the same body, except that it was now in a glorified state, He could walk through walls and be in more than one place at the same time.

The resurrection of the body is an essential Christian (and even Jewish) doctrine, as the Apostle Paul declares, "But if there is no resurrection of the dead, then Christ has not been raised; if Christ has not been raised, then our preaching is in vain and your faith is in vain. . . . If for this life only we have hoped in Christ, we are of all men most to be pitied" (1 Corinthians 15:13-14, 19). In other words, our hope is not only for our lives here on earth. This life is very short indeed! It is the next life, the one that is eternal, which we hope for.

Because, as Paul tells us, the Christian faith cannot exist without this doctrine, it has been infallibly defined by the Catholic Church. It is included in the Church's infallible profession of faith, the Apostles' Creed, and has been solemnly taught by the Church's ecumenical councils. When will all this take place? Definitely, it will occur on the last day. The Bible tells us, "For the Lord himself will descend from heaven with a cry of command, with the archangel's call, and with the sound of the trumpet of God. And the dead in Christ will rise first" (1 Thessalonians 4:16). So, the Christian should have no fear of death. All those who have followed Him have His promise that one day we, too, shall rise like Him and enjoy that heavenly bliss with Him for all eternity.

Dear Grace,

I had a friend ask me, "If God is a good God, then why does He not cure sick children? Why does He allow them to suffer?" I did not know how to answer this.

This is a question that has troubled mankind from the beginning of time. Why does God allow suffering and evil in the world? First of all, let us say that it is a mystery, and in recognizing that, we know that in this life, we will never be able to comprehend it completely.

Did God have to save us by becoming one of us and suffer and die? No, of course not. He could have done it in any way He wished. In choosing suffering, He showed us love, and yes, even joy. In Old Testament times, before Christ, suffering had no real meaning. It was thought that when people suffered, it was a punishment from God, but Jesus changed all that. He transformed suffering into love. He said there is no greater love than to lay down your life for a friend.

So, when we suffer or witness others suffering, we should not run away from it. Instead, we should run to the Cross. The Cross is the answer. If we look long and deeply enough, we will see not only a man hanging there with nails in His hands and feet. We will see love, and that love will transform us, change us, and maybe lead to even greater good in the world. People who suffer, especially innocent children, should be like lights for us in the darkness. There can always be some good that can come from it.

This does not mean that suffering is something to be enjoyed or that it is in itself good. By itself, it is not good, but God can bring from it something we never expected if we unite it to the suffering of Christ; then it has meaning. When the mind looks for evil, it will find it. When it looks for goodness and love, it will find that too. This is difficult for us to see, but we must try. The great St. Philip Neri once said, "The cross is the gift God gives to his friends."

Dear Grace,

What is the best answer to those who say that Catholics worship statues of Mary and the saints?

When confronted with this, we need to explain that Catholics worship only God. Statues are images of the persons they represent. The attention that we give to Mary and the saints is not worship but rather veneration, which is profound respect or reverence because of the holy lives they led. When we kneel in front of a painting of Mary or a statue of St. Joseph, we are not praying to the object. Instead, we are acknowledging that the person the statue represents is in heaven with God and asking him or her to pray for us.

Many of us carry pictures of our loved ones in our wallets or have them displayed in our home, and yet no one would ever think of accusing us of worshipping these people. Photographs help us to remember those persons they represent, especially those who have died. Religious statues and art likewise are meant to aid us in honoring and imitating those who led very holy lives. They are examples for us, and reminders of the kind of person we should be striving to be. Each of us is called to be a saint. And we need all the help we can get.

Dear Grace,

I know that the Catholic Church allows cremation, but could you explain under what conditions it is allowed and also how the ashes are to be treated? Is scattering of ashes in accordance with Church teaching?

Your question is one that many people were asking after the burial at sea of John F. Kennedy, Jr., in 1999. To answer this, let us consider the human body. The Church has always regarded the human body as sacred. This is because it is made in the image and likeness of God. He did not make us to be only a soul, but a body as well. We are a unity of body and soul. As Catholics, we believe that at the moment of death the body and soul will separate, but we also believe firmly that our soul is going to be reunited with our body on the last day, when Jesus returns. This helps us to understand how we are to take care of the body for burial after death.

Cremation is a custom that has been practiced since ancient times, but we see, in studying history, that it depended on the views that people had of the afterlife. The Christians never burned their dead. In fact, during the earliest times of the Church, when they were being persecuted, they often even risked their lives in order to recover the bodies of the martyrs so they could give them a Christian burial. They wanted to follow the personal example of Jesus and Jewish custom. It was those who wanted to destroy faith in the resurrection of the body who would cast the corpses of martyred Christians into the flames.

Historical evidence shows that the Church has never believed that cremating a body makes the resurrection of that body impossible. This is why today cremation is permitted, but even then, only when there is good reason and provided that it does not demonstrate a denial of faith in the resurrection of the body (see CCC, n. 2300f). It is still much more in line with the Church's teaching to bury the body in the traditional, acceptable way — in a grave, entombed in a mausoleum, or even buried at sea.

The cremated remains of the body may be properly buried at sea in the urn, coffin, or other container in which they have been carried to the place of committal. The remains must be treated the same way a body would, with reverence and honor and never be scattered on the sea, from the air, or on the ground, or kept in the home of a relative or friend of the deceased. After all, is this not a body that received the sacraments and our Lord in the Holy Eucharist when it was living? How can we not treat it with utmost reverence?

Dear Grace,

My Protestant friends say that I should only follow what the Bible says and that Catholic tradition is not from God. What do I say to them?

You need to tell them that Catholicism is not a religion of the Bible alone. This is one important area where we differ strikingly from our Protestant brothers and sisters in Christ who believe in *Sola Scriptura* — the "Bible alone" — as our authority. Jesus' last command to His Apostles before ascending into heaven was that they "go therefore and make disciples of all the nations . . . teaching them to observe all I have commanded you"; He even added a promise — "I am with you always, until the end of the world" (Matthew 28:19-20). At that point, Jesus did not give them a book to follow. That "book," which contained the New Law — the New Testament — did not even begin to be written until sometime between A.D. 50 and 100.

Therefore, what Jesus left on earth to complete His mission was the Church, guided by the Holy Spirit. It was not until the year 393 that the books of the New Testament were accepted and approved by the Catholic Church at the Council of Hippo. For nearly four hundred years, we had no written or approved New Testament. So, what or who did the Church (the followers of Christ) follow for those first four hundred years? It was the teaching of the Apostles, whom Jesus had left in charge of His Church, telling them that He would be with them to the end. This oral teaching is what the Catholic Church calls Tradition with a capital "T." It comes from the Latin word *tradere* ("to hand down"). The Apostles handed down what they received from Christ Himself, and Christ was God.

It is the firm belief of the Catholic Church that God has revealed Himself to His creation through both Sacred Tradition and Sacred Scripture, and that these are interpreted by the only authoritative and authentic interpreter of the Word of God — the Church. The Bible itself tells us that the Church is "the pillar and bulwark of the truth" (1 Timothy 3:15). Why would it say that so clearly if it were the Bible alone that we should follow? Yes, the Bible is at the heart of our faith, but we have more than only the "written" Word of God. In fact, John states for us that there are so many things that Jesus said and did, but if these were to be written down, the whole world could not contain all the books that would have to be written (see John 21:25). We are truly blessed with our rich Sacred Tradition.

Dear Grace,

Do Catholics really believe in guardian angels? What is this belief based on?

Yes, Catholics really do believe in guardian angels. Every year, the Church, in one of her most ancient feasts, sets aside October 2 to honor these angelic beings who protect us from spiritual and physical harm and inspire us to do good. We see in the Old Testament that God told Moses, "Behold I send an angel before you, to guard you on the way and to bring you to the place which I have prepared. Give heed to him and hearken to his voice . . . for my name is in him" (Exodus 23:20-21).

The Catholic Church has long believed that Jesus Himself showed us the existence of guardian angels when He said, "See that you do not despise one of these little ones; for I tell you that in heaven their angels always behold the face of my Father who is in heaven" (Matthew 18:10). More than anything, our angelic guardians are entrusted with helping us to come to know and love God in this life. This includes every human person, not just Catholics!

The guardian angels are truly our best friends on this earth, and yet, we ignore them so much. Beside each one of us stands an angel given to us by God to watch over us our whole life (see CCC, n. 336). How many times have we escaped danger and wondered in amazement how in the world it happened? Probably it was our guardian angel! We need to acknowledge them in our lives, so that they might be able to help us even more. Every mother should teach her child this beautiful prayer: "Angel of God, my guardian dear; to whom God's love commits me here. Ever this day be at my side, to light and guard, to rule and guide."

Dear Grace,

How can one truly believe in the "creation story" in the Bible when there is evidence of evolution at the Smithsonian Institute's Museum of Natural Science?

This question would lead us to think that there is some conflict between science and religion, when, in reality, there should not be. Science and religion are always after one and the same thing — the truth. And we know that One Truth to be God. The Catholic Church has never had a problem with the "theory of evolution" or any evidence of it at the Smithsonian or elsewhere. The fact is, there have been several theories of evolution, not just Darwin's. In simple terms, the theory of evolution would have us believe that man developed from lower life-forms. It usually speaks about the "process" of evolution and not origins. We should keep in mind that the Church has never taught that the first chapter of Genesis is meant to teach science. It is a religious story that tells us that God is the Creator of all things, and that is what we need to focus on.

Life is so mysterious and so is our faith. We want so much to understand. There should be no fear or worry about studying or considering the theory of evolution. In many ways, it has done much to unravel the mysteries of our development. At the same time, however, we must remember that it is a theory (an assumption based on limited information and knowledge) that has never been completely proven and may never be. The real problem comes when we begin to speak of the theory of evolution as if it were a religion of its own. Science is based on facts that must be proven before being completely accepted. Religion is based on faith and is accepted even without proof because it is revealed by God.

Our Holy Father John Paul II has stated: "The Church insists that man is not an accident; that no matter how He went about creating man, God from all eternity intended that man and all creation exist in their present form." Catholics are not obliged to square scientific data with the early verses of Genesis, and we are not opposed to any theory of natural evolution as long as it does not exclude the action of God and what we know from God's own self-revelation. We do know this: no human person was present at the Creation to record it and tell us about it today. However, Jesus Christ, as the second person of the Holy Trinity, *was present* at creation, and His very life and mission tell us that the "message" in the Book of Genesis is true.

Dear Grace,

What is the Catholic Church's teaching about purgatory? What is it based on?

Today, even among many Catholics, little mention is made of purgatory, and yet it is an essential doctrine of the Catholic Church. What this teaching basically proclaims is that those souls who die in a state of grace but have venial sins still unforgiven, as well as those who have not made up completely for the punishment due for forgiven mortal sin, will be detained in a state called purgatory for a time. In other words, all the souls in purgatory are those who died in a state of grace and are on their way to heaven but must first be purified in order to achieve the holiness necessary to enter that eternal joy with God.

The Catholic Church teaches the belief in the state of purgatory because we have the words of the Bible itself attesting to the value of prayers for the dead. We read that Judas, the commander of the forces of Israel, sent money to Jerusalem to be offered as sacrifice for the sins of the dead: "He also took up a collection . . . to provide for a sin offering. In doing this he acted very well and honorably, taking account of the resurrection. For if he were not expecting that those who had fallen would rise again, it would have been superfluous and foolish to pray for the dead. . . . Therefore he made atonement for the dead, that they might be delivered from their sin" (2 Maccabees 12:43-45). If his men who had died had gone to heaven, there would have been no need to pray for them, and if they had gone to hell, there would also be no need to pray for them, since there is no return from hell.

There are several passages in the New Testament that also point to a process of purification after death. Jesus Himself declares that "whoever says a word against the Son of man will be forgiven; but whoever speaks against the Holy Spirit will not be forgiven, either in this age or in the age to come" (Matthew 12:32). According to some of the Doctors of the Church, these words prove that in the next life some lesser, or venial, sins will be forgiven and purged away. St. Paul also writes, "If the work which any man has built on the foundation [Jesus Christ] survives, he will receive a reward. If any man's work is burned up, he will suffer loss, though he himself will be saved, but only as through fire" (1 Corinthians 3:14-15).

In the afterlife, there are three states: heaven, hell, and purgatory, with purgatory being a temporary state and heaven and hell being eternal. When we die, we will face God's judgment for the way that we lived our lives while here on this earth, and it will, at that moment, be decided where our soul shall live for all eternity. This is called the Particular, or Individual, Judgment and is something that no one can avoid. Some of the great mystics of the Church who have had visions of purgatory tell us that the pain, or fire, of that place is the separation from God. Belief in purgatory should inspire us to amend our lives while there is still time so that we will not go there, and also to pray for the souls who are there and need our prayers in order to be released and reach heaven.

Dear Grace,

I have a friend who keeps on asking me the ultimate questions: Where do we come from? Where are we going? Why are we here? I am completely at a loss in trying to answer my friend. How does the Catholic Church deal with these concerns? Does the CCC cover these questions?

It is very fitting that we reflect on these questions that have bewildered men and women for all ages. In the very first paragraph of the Prologue to the *Catechism of the Catholic Church*, we read the following: "God, infinitely perfect and blessed in himself, in a plan of sheer goodness freely created man to make him share in his own blessed life. For this reason, at every time and in every place, God draws close to man. He calls man to seek him, to know him, to love him with all his strength. He calls together all men, scattered and divided by sin, into the unity of his family, the

Church. To accomplish this, when the fullness of time had come, God sent his Son as Redeemer and Savior. In his Son and through him, he invites men to become, in the Holy Spirit, his adopted children and thus heirs of his blessed life."

If we look closely, we will see that this statement answers all of the ultimate questions and longings of the human heart and mind. We are made by God; we are made for God; and we are on a journey back to God. This is what life is all about. Many have wondered why God would do all this, knowing how sinful the world would become, and the only answer is that simple but powerful four-letter word — love. God, who is pure love, created out of love. But love, in order to be real, must be free. If you force someone to love you, then it is not real love. So, God created both the angels and mankind free, in order that they might love Him back. He wants us to share in His blessed life.

How do we know all of this? In fact, how can we know that God even exists? There are several ways. We know God exists when we gaze at the created world in nature, when we look at another human person, and finally, we know it because of the ways in which He has revealed Himself through Divine Revelation. He did this through the Sacred Scriptures as well as the Sacred Tradition that was handed down to us by the Apostles. We know by reading the Book of Genesis in the Old Testament that God made a covenant with Abraham. He said that He would be our God and we would be His people. If we would keep His commandments and live according to His ways, we would find true happiness. Apart from Him, we would never be fulfilled.

God created us to be in total happiness with Him, but we were also free to choose to love or reject Him. We know that at some point, man abused the free will given him and chose himself rather than God. Thus, sin entered the world. This was a very serious offense against God. Like freedom, another characteristic of love is justice. God requires that offenses be made right. Who, on this earth, could pay such a price? Like a merciful and loving father — in the mystery of the Incarnation — He came into the world as one of us in the person of Jesus Christ, with a mission to pay that price and save us.

The problems that exist today in our lives and in our world stem primarily from the fact that we are trying so often to be *who we are not*. And who are we? We are adopted sons and daughters of the one, true, living God. We are here on this earth to seek Him, to know Him, to love Him, and to serve Him with all our strength. The influences of the world, it seems, are constantly telling us something else. Sometimes, we lose our perspective, and we need reminders of the tremendous and infinite love that God has for us.

In sending His only begotten Son, God revealed Himself in the fullest way possible, for Jesus Christ was God Himself. This is one of the greatest mysteries of our Christian faith. In this life, we will never be able to comprehend it completely. We know, however, that one day, when we see God face to face, it will all be made clear. Our home is not this world; our home is in heaven; we have a heavenly destiny. When people ask, "Where do we come from; why are we here; and where are we going?" our answer should be: we come from God; we are here to live for God; and we are going to God.

Dear Grace,

Why do Catholics call Mary the "Mother of God"? Was she not created by God? Does this title mean that she existed before God?

It is so good that you desire to understand the Church's teaching about Mary, the one through whom Christ our Savior came into the world. New Year's Day is the day the Catholic Church celebrates the divine motherhood of Mary, which is based on the teaching of the Gospels, on the writings of the early Fathers, and on the express definition of the Church. It is a beautiful title for Mary. What many do not realize is that this is a name that Christians have been using in reference to her for almost seventeen centuries. In order to understand how we can call Mary the Mother of God, we must first realize and accept the fact that our faith is grounded in mystery. There is much we do not fully understand now, but one day we will. That which we do understand, however, comes to us from what God has revealed.

The Bible tells us that Mary "had borne a son; and . . . his name [was] Jesus" (Matthew 1:25). We also read in the Gospel of John that Jesus is the Word made flesh. The Word, who was God, assumed human nature in the womb of Mary (see John 1:14-15). We are referring here to the mystery of the Incarnation, the Word becoming flesh. Jesus Christ (the second person of the Holy Trinity, one in being with the Father) entered this world, taking on human flesh and a human soul. Jesus is true God and true man. Because we believe that Mary was truly the Mother of Jesus, and that Jesus was truly God from the first moment of His conception, then it makes perfect sense that Mary is truly the Mother of God.

We must be careful and make clear that we are not saying that Mary created the divine person of Jesus. Mary gave birth to Jesus, the God-man. When God "assumed," or "took on," a human nature, it was the result of His perfect will to do so. He chose to be born of her. Therefore, it cannot be said that Mary created God or that she existed before God. We simply mean that a woman is considered a man's mother when she has conceived and given birth to him. St. Cyril, Bishop of Alexandria, who defended this teaching, stated that "it was not that an ordinary man was born first of the Holy Virgin, on whom afterwards the Word descended. What we say is that, being united with the flesh from the womb, (the Word) has undergone birth in the flesh, making the birth in the flesh His own." Therefore, the Blessed Virgin Mary is rightly called Mother of God, or, in Greek, *Theotokos*.

Dear Grace,

As a Catholic, I would like to have a better understanding of what infallibility means. When is it that we can say the pope teaches infallibly?

The word "infallible" literally means the "inability to err." Therefore, "infallibility" is the word that the Catholic Church uses to refer to the charism (gift) that has been given by God to the Holy Father and the Magisterium (the teaching office of the Church — pope and bishops) under certain conditions. The mistake that many people make is in thinking that this means that the pope cannot ever be wrong in anything or commit errors of any sort, including personal conduct. This is not what the Church teaches at all.

The official statement on infallibility can be found in the First Vatican Council's Dogmatic Constitution on the Church of Christ (*Pastor Aeternus*). Essentially, what it says is that the pope is preserved by the Holy Spirit from error when these four conditions are present: (1) he intends to teach (2) by virtue of his supreme authority (3) on a matter of faith and morals (4) to the whole Church. His teaching act is therefore called "infallible" and the teaching that he articulates is termed "irreformable" (see Chap. 4, n. 9).

The evidence that papal infallibility is part of the Christian faith comes to us from Sacred Scripture and the Sacred Tradition of the Church. This Tradition includes, of course, the witness of many of the early Fathers, those men of great faith who documented in their writings what was believed and practiced in the early Church.

When Peter recognized Jesus as the Messiah, the Son of the living God, Jesus turned to him and declared, "I tell you, you are Peter, and on this rock I will build my Church, and the powers of death shall not prevail against it. I will give you the keys of the kingdom of heaven, and whatever you bind on earth shall be bound in heaven, and whatever you loose on earth shall be loosed in heaven" (Matthew 16:18-19). He also instructed him to feed His lambs and tend His sheep (see John 21:15-17). It is quite clear from these passages that He meant for Peter to be in charge of His Church. Peter, who had made mistakes and shown weakness, was the one Christ chose.

Another interesting and revealing biblical passage that demonstrates the divine plan that Jesus had for Peter is the one in which He says, "Simon, Simon, behold, Satan demanded to have you, that he might sift you like wheat, but I have prayed for you that your faith may not fail; and when you have turned again, strengthen your brethren" (Luke 22:31-32). Here, He was predicting Peter's denial, and yet there is a definite indication that Peter will be preserved from error in order to strengthen the others, the rest of the Church.

He certainly knew that Peter was not perfect, that he had made mistakes and would continue to do so in the future. But when it came to matters of faith and morals (which are the matters that pertain to salvation), he would always have the assistance and guidance of the Holy Spirit. Surely Christ knew that Peter would always require this help; after all, he was a sinner who would constantly need God's grace. Does it make any sense that Jesus would leave him in charge of strengthening the others and then allow him to fall into error in his teaching of the faith? Let us remember that He said the gates of hell would never prevail against His Church.

Infallibility does not mean that the pope can teach without error on any subject he chooses. Only under the four conditions stated above can he be said to teach with a guarantee of freedom from error. In reality, only God alone is infallible. No man is perfect. When the pope teaches infallibly, it is only because of the divine assistance from God, which we believe he has received. For our Holy Father, the direct successor of St. Peter, preserving the Church in the true faith is a tremendous task and responsibility, and that is why we should remember him in our prayers daily.

Dear Grace,

I have never understood why the day Jesus died a horrible, painful death on the cross is called "Good Friday." Please tell me why we call it good.

The crucifixion and death of Jesus Christ was surely the greatest single act of evil that ever occurred in the history of the human race. There has never been anything worse done than to kill the only Son of God. So, we ask ourselves, "Why did God allow that?" And why is the day that He died called "Good Friday"?

Jesus Christ, who was God Himself, went to the cross, willingly, for a reason. It was His mission. By dying, He brought about the greatest "good" that ever was — the salvation of mankind. We were on our way to destruction, but by His death He opened the gates to heaven, which had been closed after the original sin of Adam, and thus made a way for us. This is why it was "good."

Dear Grace,

I agree with the statement in one of your recent columns that Jesus went to the netherworld in order to bring back up with Him into heaven those who had died before His coming. Then you said that He gained eternal salvation for us and heaven was opened once more. I agree. Now where does purgatory fit in here? Had all in the netherworld finished their purgatory time before His crucifixion? What about those who died just before His death? Also, is purgatory considered to be "home" when we say a person has gone home after he or she just died?

Your question is a very good one, and I thank you for writing. The first thing I think we need to clarify is that your letter seems to imply that you see purgatory as some place apart from heaven or hell in which we "do time." This is not what the Catholic Church teaches about purgatory. What she does teach is this: "All who die in God's grace and friendship, but still imperfectly purified, are indeed assured of their eternal salvation; but after death they undergo purification, so as to achieve the holiness necessary to enter the joy of heaven. The Church gives the name *Purgatory* to this final purification of the elect, which is entirely different from the punishment of the damned [cf. Council of Florence (1439): DS 1304; Council of Trent (1536): DS 1820; (1547): 1580; see also Benedict XII, *Benedictus Deus* (1336): DS 1000]" (CCC, n. 1030f).

Purgatory, therefore, is not a place apart from heaven. It is a state of purification, and all who are in this state are destined for heaven. In other words, in the afterlife, there are three states but only two in which one will live out eternity, and those are heaven and hell. Heaven will be that total communion with God in the Holy Trinity (Father, Son, and Holy Spirit) and in the company of the angels, the saints, and all the blessed. Hell, on the other hand, will be the total and never-ending separation from God.

According to one traditional explanation, when a person dies, the body and soul separate. The body is buried, awaiting the final resurrection, when it will be reunited with the soul. The soul then continues its journey, to the state of heaven or hell. If the soul is in need of purification before it goes to meet God, it will first undergo that purification in the state of purgatory. How long this will be for, we do not know. Just as in heaven, in purgatory there is no time, not as we know it here on earth. God's time is not our time. What is believed to be the suffering, or "fire," of purgatory is that the souls in this state know beyond a shadow of a doubt that God exists and want nothing more than to be with Him but cannot for a while. That is the tremendous pain, the separation from God, even for a short time.

Before Jesus' coming, it was the understanding that all who had died went to the netherworld, the abode of the dead, in which there was a separation between the "damned" and the "just" — those who had died in God's grace and friendship. This separation in the netherworld is attested to in the Parable of the Rich Man and Lazarus that is found in the Gospel of Luke (16:19-31). Both Lazarus and the rich man had gone to this place, but Lazarus was with the "just," with Abraham, and the rich man with the "damned" because of the life he had lived. When he asks Abraham to have Lazarus bring him water, Abraham responds, "Between us and you a great chasm has been fixed, in order that those who would pass from here to you may not be able, and none may cross from there to us" (Luke 16:26).

It was the "just" whom Jesus descended into the netherworld to bring up into heaven. We cannot know if any of them had to be purified before entering heaven. Perhaps some did. If they did not need this purification, then we might be able to say they went straight to heaven. Keep in mind, however, that while we speak of "going" to heaven, purgatory, or hell, we are simply using words to help us describe a state of being and not a "place."

Regarding your other question about someone who dies today: Can we say that such a person has gone "home" even if he or she might have been in need of this purification? The answer is yes. This earth is not our real home; our home is in heaven, and those souls in the state of purgatory are indeed on their way there. We should remember the holy souls and know that when they reach heavenly bliss, they will remember and pray for us in return.

Dear Grace,

I love my religion and go to church and pray every day. My question is this: Who is Satan? How powerful is he? How and when was he ousted from heaven? Every time something goes wrong in my life, I always blame it on him. Am I right to believe this?

The name Satan is a Hebrew word that signifies "accuser." This corresponds with the Greek *diabolos*, which means "one who 'throws himself across' God's plan" (CCC, n. 2851). The term, over time, gradually became the proper name of the fallen angel Lucifer, whose name is from the Latin and literally means "light-bringing." He was one of the most beautiful and one of the highest of the angels that God had created.

All of the angels were created in a state of innocence and grace (see CCC, n. 391). However, before they could enter the heaven of the Blessed Trinity and see the fullness of God's glory in the Beatific Vision, it is believed that they had to undergo a trial, or test. When they were first created, they had full knowledge of God but could not yet see Him. While we may not know exactly what this test was, we do know that Lucifer, exercising the free will given to him by God, protested and thus chose himself over God. We know from Scripture that a large number of angels fell with him. They immediately turned into horrible devils and were cast out of heaven and condemned to hell for all eternity.

The reason that their sin was unforgivable is because they, unlike us, had full knowledge of God and knew exactly what they were doing. Their natures and intelligence were superior to that of any human being. Therefore, once they chose themselves over God, their sin was irrevocable (see CCC, n. 393). Now, they rage against God and all humanity. Being angels, they retained their great natures, intellect, and wills. Their love and sanctity was transformed, however, by their own sin into malice and hate, although they do still possess tremendous power and strength.

The Catholic Church has always taught the existence of Satan. Scripture tells us to "be sober, be watchful. Your adversary the devil prowls around like a roaring lion, seeking someone to devour. Resist him, firm in your faith" (1 Peter 5:8-9). The problem today is that many no longer believe in the devil, and that is precisely how he is able to tempt that person into sin. He never gives up, because his aim is to bring us totally down with him and away from God.

As far as blaming him for everything that goes wrong in your life, remember that, while he is at the root of all evil, we do still have free choice. He is unbelievably strong and cunning, but God is always stronger. In fact, without God's grace to assist us, we would never be able to resist Satan. The only reason that he has any power on this earth is because God allows it, and that is a great mystery, which will one day be revealed to us.

Dear Grace,

What does it mean when a person is excommunicated from the Catholic Church?

At Baptism, we as Christians enter into a "communion" with our Lord Jesus Christ and His Church. When we sin, it is possible to break that communion. This is what happens with serious, or mortal, sin, when one has knowingly and willingly disobeyed God. As a result, we cut ourselves off from Him. If a person repents, however, and asks forgiveness through the sacrament of Reconciliation, this communion with Christ and His Church can be restored. This is what excommunication attempts to achieve.

For the ordinary laity, canon law states that an excommunicated person is forbidden "to celebrate the sacraments and sacramentals and to receive the sacraments" (canon 1331.1.2). In most cases, the person would have to have the penalty formally pronounced by a sentence and the guilty party would not be bound to it until this had been done. There are certain offenses, however, that would incur an automatic excommunication simply by having committed the offense (see canon 1314).

Some examples of the grave offenses that would incur automatic excommunication would be the following: apostasy (total denial of the faith); heresy (denial of some truth of the faith); schism (refusal of submission to the Roman Pontiff) (see canon 1364); direct violation of the seal of confession by a priest (see canon 1388); and procuring or performing an abortion or cooperating in an abortion in a way that is necessary to its being performed (see canon 1398).

The Church realizes, of course, that there are certain factors that can remove or diminish a person's guilt, such as age (too young), ignorance of the law, lack of freedom, and several other considerations (see canon 1323). In addition, a person must know that what he or she is about to do will result in a separation from Christ and the Church. There are situations, however, when the person could have known but chose not to be informed. In that type of case, there would be some accountability to God for the offense.

We need to keep in mind that excommunication is not for the purpose of separating someone from the Church or the sacraments. Rather, it is a medicinal penalty that is imposed in order to help the sinner to repent and turn back to God and be reconciled with Him and the members of His body, the community of believers. It heals the wound caused by the sinner, who is wounded himself, as well as the Church. The excommunication will hopefully be lifted as soon as the person has repented.

Dear Grace,

Could you please explain what an "indulgence" is and how someone may obtain one?

This is a very good question because many Catholics do not have a full knowledge or understanding of what an indulgence is or how to receive one. In order to answer, we will have to discuss sin and the consequence of sin. Often we do not want to talk about punishment due to sin. It makes God seem harsh and unforgiving, but this is not so at all. In fact, the opposite is true. Our God is a loving, merciful, and forgiving Father. When we incur a consequence or punishment due to our sin, it is always a means to a true conversion of heart and the complete purification of the sinner.

Pope Paul VI stated the following: "An indulgence is a remission before God of the temporal punishment due to sins whose guilt has already been forgiven, which the faithful Christian who is duly disposed gains under certain prescribed conditions through the action of the Church which, as the minister of redemption, dispenses and applies with authority the treasury of the satisfactions of Christ and the saints" (apostolic constitution *Indulgentiarum doctrina*, Norm 1). The doctrine on indulgences is closely linked to the Church's teaching on purgatory and the communion of saints.

In order to understand the Church's practice of granting indulgences, we must first realize that mortal sin is, above all, an offense against God. It cuts off our communion with Him, and it has two consequences — eternal punishment and temporal punishment. Eternal, of course, means forever, so that refers to the possibility of hell, or eternal damnation. Temporal, on the other hand, refers to something that lasts only for a time or not eternal. In other words, even after the sin has been forgiven and communion with God has been restored, there still remains some attachment to sin and this needs to be purified either here on earth, or after death in purgatory, before the soul can go to be with God (see CCC, n. 1472).

One may ask, "Where does the indulgence come from and how is it that the Church has the power to grant indulgences?" This requires an understanding of the doctrine of the communion of saints, which teaches that there is a life beyond this one and that those who died in faithfulness to God's friendship and love have gone to be with Him in heaven.

In addition, we also believe that by their good works, the saints, including Jesus and the Blessed Virgin Mary, have earned merit, a sort of spiritual credit. The Church, by the "power of the keys" given to Peter by Christ, has authority to dispense these merits as she sees fit. When these merits are applied to the saints in purgatory, who are in a state of purification in order to enter heaven, or to the saints on earth who are still struggling to reach heaven, they have the power to remit, or wipe away, their temporal punishment due to sin.

An indulgence is partial or plenary, as it removes either part or all of the temporal punishment due to sin. If you would like to know more about indulgences and how to gain one, a very good source would be a publication authorized by Pope Paul VI that is titled *Handbook of Indulgences*. All of the prayers and practices and examples are listed there and would be too many to include here. Usually, in addition to some particular good work, the Church requires three basic conditions for obtaining an indulgence: Confession, Communion, and prayer for the Holy Father. For additional norms, one would need to consult the *Handbook*.

Indulgences may be applied to the living or the dead for the remission of temporal punishment due to sin. We should never forget to pray for the souls in purgatory or for ourselves or our loved ones. They in turn will pray for us when they have reached the glory of heaven that awaits us all.

Dear Grace,

Is it true that the Virgin Mary had other children after she had Jesus?

It is the teaching of the Catholic Church that the Blessed Virgin Mary was a virgin her entire life — a perpetual virgin. In other words, she was a virgin before, during, and after the birth of Jesus, and therefore never had other children besides her one and only Son. That she was a virgin before and during the birth of Christ can hardly be denied, since it is so clearly attested to in Scripture. How unusual it is that most people can believe that God can make it possible for a virgin to have a child, and yet some do not believe that the same woman chose to remain a virgin for her entire life, out of her love for God.

The first thing that we should recognize is that Mary was and is a woman like no other. Knowing that God chose her above all others to bring His only begotten Son into the world, how can anyone doubt that she is very special? No human being or angel or saint has ever experienced what she alone experienced. She carried in her womb the Almighty Lord of Lords, the King of Kings, Jesus Christ, the Word made flesh. She contained in her body the incomprehensible God. Does it make sense that she would then turn around and unite that same body with that of another human creature?

The major challenges to the Church's belief in Mary's perpetual virginity are based on difficult passages of the Bible itself. There are biblical verses claimed by some to explicitly affirm that Jesus had brothers, thus proving (according to them) that Mary had other children. Although we certainly do not have the space here for a complete discussion of these verses, let us look at some of the major examples. The first and most pointed to is the use of the words "brother," brethren," or "sister" as in the following verses: "While he was still speaking to the people, behold, his mother and his brethren stood outside, asking to speak to him" (Matthew 12:46) and "Is not this the carpenter, the son of Mary and brother of James and Joses and Judas and Simon, and are not his sisters here with us?" (Mark 6:3).

From a careful study of Scripture, it is quite clear that the terms "brother," "brethren," and "sister" had a considerably wide meaning and usage in the Bible. They did not always refer to a blood brother or sister. Then why were these terms used, one might ask? There was a very good reason. The languages (Hebrew and Aramaic) spoken by Jesus and His disciples did not have a word meaning "cousin" or other kinsmen, or even friends, so they conveniently used "brother" or "sister" to refer to several kinds of relatives, and even nonrelatives. There are numerous examples in the Bible of this usage, and a detailed word study would easily substantiate this.

Another problem verse is this one: "[Joseph] took his wife, but knew her not until she had borne a son; and he called his name Jesus" (Matthew 1:25). Here, some would attempt to demonstrate that the word "until" means that after Jesus' birth, Joseph did "know" (that is, have relations) with his wife, Mary. Again, we must keep in mind that the people of that day did not speak as we do today. This is but one example of how this word was used differently from the way it is today. There are many others. So, we see that these arguments, like all others that are brought forth, cannot and do not prove that Mary had other children.

From the earliest times, the Church pondered all these things about Mary and (based on Scripture and Tradition) slowly began to formulate the beliefs and teachings regarding the Mother of Jesus. Except for one serious challenge in the fourth century, all Christians believed the perpetual virginity of Mary. Even today, many non-Catholic Christians hold it to be true. The Protestant Reformer Martin Luther himself believed Mary to be a virgin her whole life (see Luther's *On the Divine Motherhood of Mary*).

Is it possible that Joseph, having been told by the angel Gabriel that Mary would give birth in a miraculous way to the long-awaited Messiah, would then desire or seek to have relations with her? We must not lose sight of the fact that the Holy Family was unlike any other family. Imagine what it would be like to have God as your son! Jesus was God. Let us understand that Mary is the woman chosen by God to be the bearer and bringer of Christ. She was different; she was special; she was and is Ever-Virgin.

Dear Grace,
When did Jesus first realize that He was the Son of God?

As Christians, we firmly believe and profess that Jesus Christ is both fully God and fully man. This is the mystery of the Incarnation — God took on or assumed human flesh and became a man. At the Council of Chalcedon in 451, the Church authoritatively declared the following: "We unanimously teach to confess one and the same Son, our Lord Jesus Christ, the same perfect in divinity and perfect in humanity, the same truly God and truly man composed of rational soul and body, the same one in being (*homoousios*) with the Father as to the divinity and one in being with us as to the humanity, like unto us in all things but sin."

This union of God and man in one person is called the "hypostatic union." It is a mystery of faith that we, being human, cannot fully understand. It means that Jesus was at the same time the Son of God and the Son of Mary; He was divine and human, and these two natures were without confusion or change, without division or separation, but also distinct. As Chalcedon also states, "He is not split or divided into two persons, but He is one and the same only-begotten, God the Word, the Lord Jesus Christ."

Because we believe, based on Divine Revelation, that Jesus assumed a human nature like ours, except sin, we therefore also believe that He possessed a human body and a human soul. In addition, we know that it is in the soul that intellect and will are rooted. What can be said, then, regarding the moment when Jesus came to the knowledge and awareness of His identity and mission as the Son of God?

If we say that Jesus had a human soul, then we must say also that this soul, which the Son of God assumed, was endowed with a true human knowledge. And this human knowledge was limited; He lived a rather normal life in the historical conditions of His time. Therefore, Jesus — as Scripture tells us — "increased in wisdom and in stature, and in favor with God and man" (Luke 2:52), and He would have learned things in the ways that human persons do, from experience (see Mark 6:38, 8:27; John 11:34; also see CCC, n. 472).

It is also important to understand, however, that this truly human knowledge of Jesus always expressed the divine life of His person — His divine nature. "The human nature of God's Son, not by itself but by its union with the Word, knew and showed forth in itself everything that pertains to God" (St. Maximus the Confessor, *Qu. et dub.* 66: PG 90, 840A). We know this especially because of the intimate and immediate knowledge that He had of His Father — He knew who His Father was and that He was the Son, the Son of God (see Mark 14:36; Matthew 11:27; John 1:18; 8:55). In addition, Christ in His human knowledge also showed His divine ability in the way that He was able to look into the secret thoughts of human hearts — He knew what people were thinking (see Mark 2:8; John 2 25; 6:61; also see CCC, n. 473).

It was because Jesus was always united to the divine wisdom in the Person of the Word Incarnate that He would have always also had, in His human knowledge, a full understanding of the eternal plans He had been sent to fulfill — He knew and understood His mission (see Mark 8:31; 9:31; 10:33-34; 14:18-20, 26-30). For those who are concerned with what He did not know, we can say this: Whatever He might have claimed not to know or had limited knowledge of, He clearly stated elsewhere He was not sent to reveal. In other words, anything He did not know, He did not need to know. And anything He did not reveal, He was not meant to reveal (see Mark 13:32; Acts 1:7; also see CCC, n. 474).

The God-man experienced joy and sorrow, hunger, thirst, love, loneliness and even anger. He grew daily in acquiring knowledge. But He always knew who He was — the only Son of God, who had come into a sinful world in order to unite Himself to it and offer Himself in sacrifice for its salvation.

2
Church History

⁂

Dear Grace,

What are the differences between the Eastern Orthodox Church and the Roman Catholic Church?

In the history of Christianity, there has been a long-running schism — a separation from the unity of the Church, and thus also from communion — that has divided the Eastern Orthodox and Western Roman Catholic Churches. The Eastern Orthodox Church is the broad name given to the churches of the Christian East, which separated from communion with the Holy See (Rome) in a formal break in 1054, although events had been leading to it for many centuries.

The causes for this separation can be traced to the wide differences that had developed between the East and West in matters of culture, politics, jurisdiction, language, and some elements of doctrine. Among the major differences that can be noted today is that the Eastern Orthodox Churches do not recognize the primacy of the pope. The wide communion of Orthodox Churches are self-governing and under the authority of patriarchs. Chief among them is the Patriarch of Constantinople. He is considered the first among equals and does not rule over the other churches.

Another matter that sets them apart is that they do not accept the *Filioque* clause in the Nicene Creed, which states that the Holy Spirit "proceeds from the Father *and* the Son." The Orthodox hold that the Holy Spirit proceeds from the Father *through* the Son.

The Catholic Church recognizes as valid all of the Orthodox sacraments as well as the ordination and consecration of Orthodox priests and bishops. She also respects the East's many contributions and especially their mutual abiding love for the Mother of God. In the time since the Eastern Schism, a few parts of the Eastern Churches have returned to communion with the Western Roman Catholic Church and still retain the practice of the Eastern Byzantine Rite. Our Holy Father John Paul II has striven for better relations with the Christian East, and it should be every Christian's hope and prayer that one day full communion will be restored so that we might again worship together at the one table of the Lord.

Dear Grace,

Could you please explain the history or the meaning behind the Advent wreath? How was this custom started?

The origins of the Advent wreath are found in the folk practices of the pre-Christian Germanic peoples who, during the cold December darkness of Central Europe, gathered wreaths of evergreen and lighted fires as signs of hope in a coming spring and renewed light. Christians kept these popular traditions alive, and by the sixteenth century, Catholics and Protestants throughout Germany used these symbols to celebrate their Advent hope in Christ, the everlasting light. From Germany, the use of the Advent wreath spread to other parts of the Christian world.

Traditionally, the wreath is made of four candles in a circle of evergreens. Three candles are purple and the fourth is rose or pink. Each day at home, the candles are lighted, perhaps before the evening meal, one candle the first week, and then another each succeeding week until December 25. A short prayer may accompany the lighting. The advent wreath should be used to remind Catholics and other Christians about the spiritual "cold and darkness" experienced by humanity as it awaited the birth of God's Word on earth.

Dear Grace,

When and why did celibacy become required of priests in the Catholic Church?

Many people want to know, "Why can't a Catholic priest get married?" Sometimes people ask this because they might think that the life of a priest looks lonely and they are concerned for him. This kind of thinking, however, stems from a lack of understanding about the priesthood. Perhaps we are looking too much at the law and not seeing celibacy as a "gift." We miss something when we do that. To abandon everything for Christ is truly a call from God. This in no way means that it will always be easy, but then no true vocation is always so.

Celibacy, which describes the state of being unmarried, has been an issue in the Church throughout her history, and there has been much misunderstanding, especially in recent times. The law requiring a celibate clergy developed over centuries. However, historical documents clearly show that not only is the ideal of celibacy found in the Gospels, but that it was practiced from the very beginning of the Church.

Though some of the Apostles had wives, they never lived with them as husband and wife once they began to follow Christ, and we see also that the wife of a priest was referred to as his "sister." In a recent definitive study, Cardinal Alfons Stickler maintains that celibacy is a mandate from Christ Himself, and the Church can only obey it, not change it. Even though the Eastern Orthodox Churches allow their priests to marry, their bishops must be celibate. This shows that celibacy has always been part of the Tradition.

Jesus pointed out to His followers that "there is no man who has left house or wife or brothers or parents or children, for the sake of the kingdom of God, who will not receive manifold more in this time, and in the age to come eternal life" (Luke 18:28-30). One can almost imagine that the Apostles began to see that in emphasizing the putting aside of all things to follow Him, Jesus was saying that celibacy was required for Gospel ministry. But, because He did not absolutely command it, it was up to the Church to eventually decide. This, of course, happened slowly.

We have evidence that from the beginning of the fourth century, the Church of the West strengthened, spread, and confirmed this practice, which is shown in the documents of various provincial councils and through the supreme pontiffs. More than anyone else, the popes promoted, defended, and restored ecclesiastical celibacy in successive eras of history. The obligation of celibacy was then solemnly sanctioned by the Sacred Ecumenical Council of Trent and finally included in the Code of Canon Law.

The Second Vatican Council's *Presbyterorum Ordinis* ("Decree on the Ministry and Life of Priests") states that the ultimate foundation for celibacy is the "mystery of Christ and his mission." In the ordained priesthood, a man is called in a very particular way to imitate Christ and continue His mission. With time, the Church came to believe strongly that a celibate way of life is the best way for a man to fulfill this holy vocation. It is indeed a call from God Himself, and it is not meant for everyone. What many people sadly misunderstand is that celibacy is a gift, and a man freely accepts it by his own choice when he answers his call to the ministry of Christ.

Pope Paul VI wrote so beautifully, "At times loneliness will weigh heavily on the priest, but he will not for that reason regret having generously chosen it. Christ, too, in the most tragic hours of His life was alone — abandoned by the very ones whom He had chosen and whom He had loved 'to the end' — but He stated, 'I am not alone, for the Father is with me.'" So, there is no need to feel sorry for a priest. He is completely devoted to his beloved, the love of his life — Jesus!

Dear Grace,

I am curious about how the devotion of the Stations of the Cross began. Could you please explain this?

Indeed, one of the most beautiful ways to prepare for the glorious Resurrection of our Lord Jesus Christ at Easter is the Stations of the Cross. This devotion goes back to the earliest times of the Church and has evolved over time. The object of the stations is to help the faithful to make, in spirit, a pilgrimage to the major scenes of Christ's suffering and death. Today, it has become one of the most popular of Catholic devotions. It is carried out by passing from station to station, with certain prayers at each and devout meditation on the various events of Jesus' Passion.

Although it cannot be confirmed, it is believed that the Blessed Virgin Mary made daily visits to the places where her beloved Son suffered so much for the sins of the world. This should not be difficult to believe. What mother would not have done so? History shows that ever since the Roman Emperor Constantine made Christianity legal in 312, people have been making this spiritual pilgrimage. Constantine's own mother, St. Helena, was among the first to do so. St. Jerome (342-420), living in Bethlehem during the latter part of his life, also writes of the crowds of pilgrims from various countries who visited those holy places and followed the Way of the Cross or *Via Dolorosa* (Sorrowful Way), as it was later called.

Because many pilgrims could not actually travel to the Holy Land owing to the control of the area by Muslim Turks, we see that, as early as the fifth century, an interest arose to "reproduce" the holy places in other lands. One of the first examples of this is the monastery of San Stefano at Bologna, where a group of connected chapels was constructed that were intended to represent the more important shrines of Jerusalem. Eventually, reproductions of these were erected at popular spiritual centers.

William Wey, an English pilgrim, visited the Holy Land in 1462, and is credited with the term "stations." At the end of the seventeenth century, the erection of these stations in churches became more popular when Pope Innocent XI granted the right to place them in churches and also that indulgences be given for practicing the devotion as if one had been on an actual pilgrimage. Some years later, Pope Clement XII permitted stations to be created in all churches and fixed the number at fourteen.

To this day, there are fourteen traditional stations: (1) Pilate Condemns Christ to Death; (2) Jesus Carries the Cross; (3) The First Fall; (4) Jesus Meets His Blessed Mother; (5) Simon of Cyrene Helps to Carry the Cross; (6) Veronica Wipes the Face of Jesus; (7) The Second Fall; (8) Jesus Speaks to the Women of Jerusalem;

(9) The Third Fall; (10) Jesus Is Stripped of His Garments; (11) Jesus Is Nailed to the Cross; (12) Jesus Dies on the Cross; (13) Jesus Is Taken Down from the Cross; and (14) Jesus Is Laid in the Tomb. Because of the link between the Passion and death of our Lord with His Resurrection, many devotional booklets now include a fifteenth station, which commemorates the Resurrection.

A plenary indulgence (total remission from temporal punishment due to one's sins) is granted to those who piously recite the Stations of the Cross. If the person does the stations in a public place, he or she should actually move from station to station; but if the person is unable to do so because of the number of people, the person leading the devotion must do so. In addition, three conditions must also be met (preferably on the same day, but at least several days before or after): sacramental Confession, Eucharistic Communion, and prayer for the pope's intentions (see *Handbook of Indulgences*, n. 63). Those who are not able to visit a church may gain the same indulgence by piously reading and meditating on the Passion and death of our Lord for fifteen minutes. Knowing all this, let us walk with the Lord on his way to Calvary and help Him carry His cross!

Dear Grace,

What is the story behind the door at the Vatican that is opened only every twenty-five years and bricked closed in between? I am sure that many Catholics, as well as non-Catholics, would like to know its history.

The door that you are referring to is the Holy Door of the Holy Year of Jubilee. The opening and closing of this "holy door" at the beginning and end of the year of Jubilee in each of the four great basilicas in Rome is probably the most distinctive feature in the celebration of the Jubilee. The term "jubilee year" is of Hebrew origin (Old Testament), meaning "ram" or "the horn of a ram," and eventually came to refer to "the day of the blowing of the horn," or the "feast of the new year." This year was announced to the people by the blowing of the horn. As told in Scripture, the Jubilee year was the year that followed immediately seven successive Sabbatic years (the seventh year of a seven-year cycle). Therefore, the Jubilee year took place at the end of seven times seven years, that is, at the end of every forty-nine years, or the fiftieth (see Leviticus 25).

The use of the ram's horn to announce the year of Jubilee brought with it the whole notion of rejoicing. It was a time of joy, a year of remission or universal pardon. In Ezekiel 46:17, the Jubilee year is called "the year of liberty." Thus, part of the Law of the Old Testament was that each fiftieth year was to be celebrated as a Jubilee year, and that at this season every household should recover its absent members, the land return to its former owners, the Hebrew slaves be set free, and debts be remitted. These are the ideas, although somewhat later changed, that eventually shaped the Christian Jubilee, which is commonly believed to have been instituted by Pope Boniface VIII in the year 1300. It is a year in which God bestows many graces. Unlike the year of Jubilee of the Old Law, Boniface intended that it be celebrated every one hundred years, but by 1350, he decided to change it to fifty years. This was later modified to thirty-three years by Pope Urban VI and finally to twenty-five years by Pope Paul II. With very few exceptions due to political disturbances, it has remained this way since the year 1450.

The connection of a "holy door" with the celebration of the Jubilee first appears in 1423 when Pope Martin V, at the Basilica of St. John Lateran, opened the Holy Door for the first time. Pope Alexander VI later desired the Holy Door to be opened at the other Roman basilicas as well: St. Peter's, St. Mary Major, and St. Paul-Outside-the-Walls. The ritual (although it has undergone modifications) originally included the striking down (at the opening) and rebuilding (at the closing) of the wall covering the Holy Door by the Holy Father. In the ritual used for the Great Jubilee of 2000, however, there was first a demolition of the wall covering the door in a rite called the *Recognitio*. Then, at the Rite of Opening on Christmas Eve 1999, the pope opened the first door at St. Peter's himself by pushing its sides with both his hands and then closed it a year later.

In the papal bull *Incarnationis Mysterium*, John Paul II explains the importance of the Holy Door and the Great Jubilee of the Year 2000: The sign of the *Holy Door* "evokes the passage from sin to grace which every Christian is called to accomplish. Jesus said: 'I am the door' (John 10:7), in order to make it clear that no one can come to the Father except through him. This designation, which Jesus applies to himself, testifies to the fact that he alone is the Savior sent by the Father. There is only one way that opens wide the entrance into the life of communion with God: this is Jesus, the one and absolute way to salvation. To him alone can the words of the Psalmist be applied in full truth: 'This is the door of the Lord where the just may enter' (Psalm 118:20)."

Dear Grace,

Why did the Christian Church change the Sabbath from Saturday to Sunday? As you well know, the Jewish people still recognize Saturday as their Sabbath.

The Sabbath, which means "cessation" or "rest" in Hebrew, was the seventh day of the week, which the Hebrews — later known as the Jews — were commanded by God to keep holy. All work was forbidden, and violations of the Sabbath could be punishable by death. It was a day that was to be totally dedicated to God and was a sign of the Covenant that He had made with His people, Israel. "You shall keep my sabbaths, for this is a sign between me and you throughout your generations, that you may know that I, the LORD, sanctify you" (Exodus 31:13).

The strict observance of the Sabbath was, for at least the first twenty years, very much a part of the early Christian Church. Jesus, of course, was Himself a Jew — as were all His first followers — and, like them, practiced all the Jewish customs. We learn, however, that during Jesus' short public ministry, the Jewish leaders, who did not recognize Him for who He was, publicly criticized Him for violation of the Sabbath. As the Savior whom they had long awaited, He was ushering in a New Covenant, but they did not know it. Thus, when accused of nonobservance of the Saturday Sabbath, He could say to them, "The sabbath was made for man, not man for the sabbath; so the Son of man is lord even of the sabbath" (Mark 2:27-28). In other words, He could change the Sabbath because He was Lord over it; He was God.

After Jesus died, rose from the dead, and ascended to heaven, His believers, who loved Him so much, wanted to be devotedly faithful to Him and do as He had commanded. Although He had established a Church and a leader to rule and guide in His name (see Matthew 16:18-19), He had not given to them a ready set of instructions, other than to go out and preach the Good News and to follow the Holy Spirit who would lead them into all truth. There were no church buildings, no New Testament, no liturgical rites. These were left for the Church to develop, with His authority.

At the beginning, because they were still Jewish or Judaized Gentiles, the followers of "The Way," as the early believers were called (see Acts 18:25, 19:9), continued to go on the seventh day of the week for the Temple worship and observe the Sabbath. A significant change had taken place in their lives, however, and this would lead to a period of searching and wondering how they were to live as Jews and at the same time follow Jesus. They now saw Christ as the fulfillment of the Old Covenant, although they still considered themselves Jewish.

These believers in Jesus were first called Christians at Antioch (see Acts 11:26). They would meet in their homes "on the first day of the week" (Sunday) for the "breaking of the bread" (see Acts 20:7). This is what they had been commanded to do by the Lord Jesus on the night of His Last Supper (see Luke 22:19). With time, their new ways of worship, which were moving them farther and farther away from Judaism, came to the attention of the non-Christian Jewish leaders and the Roman Empire, who saw them as a threat. This led to the widespread persecution of the "Jesus Movement," a group they thought to be a temporary cult that would soon be wiped out. To their great surprise, the complete opposite happened. Against all odds, this small band of believers grew to eventually become the religion of the existing entire Western world.

Under the guidance of the Holy Spirit, and with the authority given to them by Christ, the Apostles eventually replaced the Saturday Sabbath as the day that was to be dedicated to God and changed it to Sunday, the Lord's Day. There is strong evidence in Scripture and numerous early Christian writings that Sunday was chosen because it was on that day that Jesus had risen from the dead. For example, St. Ignatius, in his Letter to the Magnesians (n. 9), speaks of Christians as "no longer observing the Sabbath, but living in the observance of the Lord's Day, on which also Our Life rose again." In the Epistle of Barnabas (n. 15) we read: "Wherefore, also, we keep the eighth day (i.e. the first of the week) with joyfulness, the day also on which Jesus rose again from the dead." Without the Easter Resurrection there would have been no faith, for it was on that day of the week that Jesus had proven He was God.

Dear Grace,

I enjoy your column very much and have learned much from you. Could you please answer a question that has puzzled me all my life? Since Jesus and many of His early followers were Jewish, how and when did the term "Roman Catholic," as we now have it, begin? Who introduced the term, and how did we change from being Jewish to being Roman Catholic?

It is a well-documented historical fact that Christianity was a middle-Eastern religion that eventually spread to the West. The "Jesus Movement," or "The Way," as it was first called, began in Galilee and later was centered in Jerusalem because it was there that Jesus did most of His preaching and where He died. Many of His first disciples were thus Jewish. Before ascending to heaven, Jesus gave to His Apostles the command to go out and teach the Good News to all the nations (see Matthew 28:19-20). It is thus clear that Christ meant that the whole world should know about

Him and come to salvation. This would, of course, mean that the Christian faith (which would later be called "Catholic") would eventually have to move far beyond the borders of Israel and the Jewish faith, where it had begun.

Among the Jews during this time were two groups that were at odds with each other: the conservative Aramaic-speaking Jews and the more liberal-minded Greek-speaking Jews. Many of these Greek-speaking Jews accepted the new "Way" and became believers in Jesus. This caused the tensions between the two groups to intensify, which eventually resulted in the conservative Jews driving the more liberal Greek-speaking Jewish followers of Jesus out of Jerusalem. They fled to Antioch, and it was from here that Christianity was launched into the entire Western and Eastern world. This was in large part due to the missionary activity of the Apostle Paul (see Acts 13:1-3). They were now called Christians. Judaism receded more and more into the background. Much of the story of how the Christian faith spread and grew is found in the Acts of the Apostles.

The word "catholic" comes from the Greek word *katholikos*, which means "throughout the world," or "universal." There are many examples in the writings of the early Church Fathers that clearly show how the word very soon came to be used to describe the Church that Jesus Christ had founded on St. Peter (see Matthew 16:18-19) and the Apostles. Our first documented evidence comes from the letter of St. Ignatius to the Smyrnaeans, written about the year 110. He writes, "Wheresoever the bishop shall appear, there let the people be, even as where Jesus may be, there is the [*katholike*] Church." There are numerous examples of this usage, and it shows how "Catholic" soon became the proper name of the Church founded by Christ.

How the Church came to be called "Roman Catholic" rests on the fact that Peter made his way to Rome and was later martyred there. It was clear to the followers of Christ that He had chosen Peter to be the leader, or head, of the Church. He had given to him "the keys to the kingdom of heaven" (Matthew 16:19) and had entrusted him with feeding His lambs (see John 21:15-17). In Scripture, only the Messiah and the Apostle Peter are spoken of as having this authority. Isaiah 22:22 reads, "And I will place on his shoulder the key of the house of David; he shall open, and none shall shut; and he shall shut, and none shall open." In all countries the "key" is the symbol of authority. Thus, Christ's words were a promise that He would confer on Peter supreme power to govern the Church. Peter was to be His vicar, to rule in His place.

Peter was recognized, from the time of the early Church, as having a position of primacy. He was the first Bishop of Rome and his successors would inherit his supremacy over the Church. The term "Roman Catholic Church" is thus based upon the fact that Rome is the central place of the Bishop of Rome who is the head of the Catholic Church founded by Jesus Christ.

Dear Grace,

If Jesus and His first followers were Jewish and we are all Christians who want to be Christ-like, why aren't we Messianic Jews? Why don't we follow the Jewish traditions?

First, we must understand who Messianic Jews are. For centuries, being Jewish has been equated with being non-Christian. Today, the movement called Messianic Judaism has changed all of that. Messianic Jews are Jews who have come to believe that Yeshua (the Hebrew name for Jesus) is the promised Messiah of Israel and, at the same time, maintain their Jewish identity and worship style. Because many are not familiar with this movement, it seems unusual to hear of Jews who believe in Jesus. You ask why we are not Messianic Jews? History tells the story.

A Christian is a believer and follower of Jesus Christ, the only Son of God, who died for our sins and rose from the dead, proving that He was God. Yes, Jesus and His first followers were Jewish, and yes, we as Christians want to be Christ-like, but we know from historical and scriptural evidence that what began originally as a Jewish Christian faith in Jerusalem was rejected by the nonbelieving Jews. Thus, the Gospel of Jesus Christ was preached to the Gentiles (non-Jews) and eventually to the whole world (see Acts 13:44-52). In attempting to survive, however, the early Christian Church found itself being pushed farther and farther away from Judaism.

In the Book of Acts, Luke records for us the story of the events that changed the course of the history of the Christian people forever. Because of the manner in which the new "Way" was being preached to the Gentiles, many of the Jewish people feared that Christianity was a threat to their own cultural heritage and were therefore suspicious of Paul and his message. But the Spirit of God was always with the Church. Jesus Himself had declared to Peter, "I tell you, you are Peter [from the Greek *petros*, meaning "rock"] and on this rock I will build my church, and the powers of death shall never prevail against it" (Matthew 16:18). The Church founded on Peter would never perish.

For the first three hundred years, the Christian Church experienced severe persecutions at the hands of the Roman emperors, who saw them as a threat to the State. Many were martyred for the faith. Some were crucified, boiled in hot oil, fed alive to lions, or decapitated. But the faith never died. As time went on, the believing Jewish Christians were excluded from the synagogues, but they took their Jewish traditions with them and adapted them as they continued to develop a form of worship that was patterned after the Jewish synagogue service. And always, they looked to Peter, guided by the Holy Spirit, for leadership and teaching.

Without a doubt, one of the greatest single events that led to the ultimate predominance of the Christian Church (which was by that time already called "Catholic") was the signing of the Edict of Milan in 313 by the Roman Emperor Constantine. Although he did not officially become a Christian until on his deathbed, he had become attracted to Christianity and thus moved to legalize it, making it the official religion of the Roman Empire. It is unfortunate, however, that because Constantine was so strongly anti-Jewish, the relations between Jews and Christians became even more strained. There eventually came a time when being Jewish and being Christian were considered to be contradictory.

Today, some Jews are accepting Jesus as their Savior, and we are seeing Messianic Jewish communities springing up. There are still, however, major differences. Messianic Jews, unlike Jews who have converted to Catholicism, do not yet, for example, recognize the Roman Pontiff, John Paul II, as the head of the Church that Jesus Christ founded. So, while we may not yet be in communion, we share some beliefs in common and pray for the day when we will be one Body in Christ.

3
Scripture

Dear Grace,

Why do Catholics call priests "father" when Christ said, "Call no man your father on earth, for you have one Father, who is in heaven" (Matthew 23:9)?

This is a clear case of taking a Scripture passage very literally on one's own interpretation instead of that of the Church, which the Bible states is "the pillar and bulwark of the truth" (1 Timothy 3:15). For example, Jesus also said, "If your right eye causes you to sin, pluck it out and throw it away; it is better that you lose one of your members than that your whole body be thrown into hell" (Matthew 5:28). Did Jesus mean for us to take this literally? If He did, then most of us would be blind, wouldn't we? Of course, that is not what He meant. Therefore, it is very possible that when He said, "Call no man your father," He also meant something else.

When Jesus said in this passage to "call no man father, master, or rabbi," He was issuing a command not to seek teachers other than God. Their teachings and traditions should not replace the Law of God as the Pharisees did. The passage is also a charge against those who seek power for the earthly pleasures that it offers. Clearly, the entire chapter is a condemnation of the practice of the Pharisees. They were the teachers (spiritual fathers) of the day, but they erred because they exchanged the teachings of God for the teachings of men. The Pharisees named their own teachers as the ultimate fathers. They fed on their own spiritual food and no longer sought God's perfect food. They elevated their teachings over the Law of God.

We find that the word "father" is used in the New Testament to mean a teacher of spiritual things, someone by whom the soul of man is born again into the likeness of Christ (see 1 Corinthians 4:14-15; 2 Corinthians 12:14; 1 John 2:1; 3 John 4; Galatians 4:19). The Apostles are called "fathers" in the New Testament and they referred to fellow Christians who were not their natural offspring as children or sons (see 1 Peter 5:13; 1 John 2:1; 1 Corinthians 4:15, 17; 1 Timothy 1:2, 18; 2 Timothy 1:2). They called themselves "fathers" because they fulfilled the biblical requirements of being a father. They formed churches and people; they fed churches and they maintained them.

By preaching the Word of God, the Apostles continued the work of showing forth the Fatherhood of God to the rest of the world. Today, the Catholic Church teaches that the bishop or priest "images" this same "fatherhood." They bring us into the Church by Baptism; they feed us the Word of God and the sacrament of Holy Communion, and by doing this they maintain us in the Church. St. Paul himself instructed Timothy and Titus in the requirements for priest by telling them that they should be good "fathers" (see 1 Timothy 3:4-5; Titus 1:6).

Dear Grace,

What is meant by the "rapture"? Where is this found in the Bible?

"Rapture" — which is not a term used by most Catholics — refers to an event that will take place at the end of time when Christ returns at the Second Coming. According to this doctrine, when Jesus appears, all of those who have died in God's friendship will be raised and transformed into a glorious state, along with those who are still on earth, and then they will all be raised up to be with Him.

The key text referring to the rapture is 1 Thessalonians 4:16-17, which states: "For the Lord himself will descend from heaven with a cry of command, with the archangel's call, and with the sound of the trumpet of God. And the dead in Christ will rise first;

then we who are alive, who are left, shall be caught up together with them in the clouds to meet the Lord in the air; and so we shall always be with the Lord." Instead of the word "rapture," however, the Catholic Church refers to this event as "the resurrection of the dead."

Much of the discussion about the rapture seems to focus on when it is going to happen. Scripture verses are often used in an attempt to figure out the hour, and this has led to much confusion and disappointment. The Church does not worry about this because she knows that no one but God knows the hour or the day of the Second Coming. It is far better to live every day as if it were our last and be prepared to meet Jesus on the day of His return, and then to be found worthy to live with Him for all eternity. As we approached the Third Millennium much talk about the rapture and the end times was being emphasized by the secular world. However, we, as Christians, rejoiced as we approached the year 2000, as it was a year of Jubilee. It was a year of celebrating — the birth of Jesus Christ as Lord and Savior.

Dear Grace,

I have always wanted to know where the title "Catholic" came from. Where in the Holy Bible do you find the name "catholic"?

Thank you for your letter because it gives us a chance to answer a question that many ask. The word "catholic" comes from the Greek word *katholikos*, which means "throughout the world" or "universal." Many classic Greek and early Christian writers used it in this general sense in order to contrast something that was *merikos* (partial) or *idios* (particular). One example of this is found in the Bible in the ancient phrase "Catholic Epistles" as applied to those of St. Peter and St. Jude. They were so called because they were addressed not to particular local communities but to the Church at large.

With time, the word "catholic," as it has happened with many other words, came to refer to something specific because of the way it was used. There are many examples in the writings of the early Church Fathers that clearly demonstrate how the word very soon came to be used to describe the Church Jesus Christ had founded on St. Peter and the Apostles. Our first documented evidence comes from the letter of St. Ignatius to the Smyrnaeans, written about the year 110. He writes: "Wheresoever the bishop shall appear, there let the people be, even as where Jesus may be, there is the [*katholike*] Church."

Clement of Alexandria also speaks very clearly: "We say," he declares, "that both in substance and in seeming, both in origin and in development, the primitive and Catholic Church is the only one, agreeing as it does in the unity of one faith." There are so many examples of this usage and it shows how "Catholic" soon became the proper name, in other words, of the true Church founded by Christ.

You ask where in the Bible the name "catholic" appears. The name does appear, as I stated above, but not as a proper name. However, it is not necessary for the Church to have been given her formal name in the Bible for that to be her name. After all, keep in mind that when Jesus left this earth in bodily form, the New Testament had not yet even been written.

As pointed out elsewhere in this book, Jesus' last command to His Apostles before ascending into heaven was that they "go therefore and make disciples of all the nations . . . teaching them to observe all I have commanded you." He even made this promise — "I am with you always, until the end of the world" (Matthew 28:19-20). Our Lord did not provide His followers a "book of instructions" to follow. That "book," which contained the New Law (the New Testament), would not be compiled until several years after Jesus' Ascension, specifically between the years 50 and 100.

Therefore, what Jesus left to complete His mission on this earth was the Church, guided by the Holy Spirit. And the Church was for everyone — universal — catholic! It was not until the year 393 that the canonical books of the New Testament were accepted and approved by the Catholic Church at the Council of Hippo. For nearly four hundred years we had no official New Testament. So, what or *who* guided the Church (the followers of Christ) for those first four hundred years? It was the teaching of the Apostles, whom Jesus had left in charge of His Church, telling them that He would be with them to the end.

When a baby is born and then given a name, it does not change anything about *who* the baby "is." He or she simply has a name now, something to be called or to go by. Likewise, the Church was Catholic since the day she was born, on the cross, when water and blood flowed from Jesus' side. The Church acquired her name with time, but this changes nothing about who or what she was from the beginning and still is today. The Church is Catholic — universal — and she wishes that all should enter and be saved. That is what Jesus wanted — one Body in Christ.

Dear Grace,

During Lent, my eight-year-old son and I were watching *Jesus Christ Superstar* and he asked me, "Was Judas the bad guy?" Out of the mouths of children come the most profound questions. Can you help me to answer his question?

Yes, indeed, children ask the most interesting questions, and this is good in that it makes us stop and think about things we might not ordinarily give our time to. If we think about it carefully, it seems that when children, or even adults, speak about the "bad guy" or the "good guy," what it boils down to is a question regarding sin or sinfulness. What is really being asked is whether or not what the person did was right or wrong. Judas's betrayal of Jesus, which directly brought about His condemnation, crucifixion, and death, was most definitely not good, although, from it, God brought about a great good — our salvation. Not only that, but it became one of the most mysterious sins of all time. So, yes, we could say, in a sense, that he is the "bad guy," but there is more to it than that. Let us look at this more closely.

Over the centuries, Judas's betrayal has been the topic of many debates and the subject of numerous studies. Some of these have gone to extremes, at times portraying him to be far more evil than he was, while others paint him as an innocent one who was merely used by God in order to have the prophecies about Jesus fulfilled. The Scriptures do not tell us very much about his history. One rather interesting thing to note, however, is that in all the texts that mention Judas, it is never done without some reference to his great betrayal (see Matthew 10:4; Mark 3:19; Luke 6:16; John 6:71). In this, no doubt, the Gospel shows us that he played a very definite role in our salvation story, but it was a role that he himself chose.

We know from the accounts in Matthew and Mark that Judas acted out of his own free will in handing Jesus over to the chief priests (see Matthew 26:14-15; Mark 14:10-11). You will notice in these that no one forces him to go to them asking for money in exchange for giving Him up. He initiates the action himself. Judas was not an innocent person used by God to do evil, especially to His only begotten Son. Love (which is equated with God) demanded justice, and when Jesus made the free choice to go to the cross and pay the price for our sins, then the crucifixion became necessary. God does not create evil, nor evilness in people, but rather He takes it and, by His power and love and mercy, transforms it into good.

The part that Satan played in Judas's betrayal is also evident from the biblical texts (see John 13:2). In Judas, we see how weak we can become under the devil's temptations. The good news for him, however, and a lesson for us, is that he repented of what he had done. The Scripture says, in fact, that he was so remorseful, after realizing what he had done, he went out and committed suicide by hanging himself (see Matthew 27:3-5), which, of course, was wrong.

What a good father you are to seek answers for your son. Perhaps you can explain to him that we should never judge the person but instead judge the sin. We need to remember that Judas was chosen by the Lord as one of the Twelve Apostles. This means that he walked with Jesus during His short ministry and was directly exposed to His great teachings about love, mercy, and forgiveness. None of the Apostles was without sin. After all, Peter denied the Lord three times and yet he was forgiven, and, in fact, was given the keys to the Kingdom!

Perhaps we could say that Judas is the "bad guy" who, in the end, did the right thing. He tried to give the money back, but it was too late. Even though God knows in advance the actions we will take in life, it is still we who make those choices and sometimes they are the wrong ones, but the wonderful thing is that He is always ready to forgive. All we must do is ask.

Dear Grace,

Was the Garden of Eden a heavenly or an earthly place?

In the Genesis account of creation in Sacred Scripture, we read that after He created the heavens and the earth, God created man and woman and then "the LORD God planted a garden in Eden, in the east; and there he put the man whom he had formed" (Genesis 2:8). According to this, it would seem to indicate that the Garden of Eden could have been a place on earth. Some modern archaeologists have hypothesized where Eden may have been located. Evolutionists, who do not accept the Genesis account of the creation story, of course would not agree with this, but archaeology also has had something to say on the matter.

Influenced solely on evidence furnished by excavations, some modern archaeologists appear to be in agreement that Mesopotamia, which is the area of modern-day Iraq, was the location of the place where the human race first appeared on earth. They base this opinion on their scientific findings, but it happens to agree with the story in the Book of Genesis, which says that the Garden of Eden was watered by the Phison, the Gehon, the Tigris, and the Euphrates. Today, only the Tigris and Euphrates rivers still retain their ancient names. For some archaeologists, this information is enough to assume that, according to the biblical account, the Garden of Eden was located somewhere in Mesopotamia, but, again, this is still hypothesis.

Dear Grace,

Why do you suppose Lucifer was allowed into Paradise?

Lucifer, who is most often referred to as Satan or the devil, is an angel who was created originally good by God. Because he chose himself over God, however, he was cast out from heaven. Throughout Scripture, we see a conflict that is waged on earth between good and evil. There is no doubt that Satan has been allowed to roam about the earth from the beginning. Jesus even referred to him as "the ruler of this world" (John 12:31, 14:30, 16:11). But it is always made clear that it is only because God allows it (see Job 1:6-12).

In the second and third chapters of the Book of Genesis, we read the story of Paradise (the Garden of Eden) and the test of free will. We all know the story so well and we know from many scriptural references that the tempter was Satan. There is always a nagging question, though. Why did God allow him there? Throughout the ages, men have wondered why God created us at all if He knew exactly what would happen. Deep meditation and thought lead us to the great mystery of love and what love is.

God, who is pure love itself, created everything out of love. But love, in order to be real, must be free. If love is forced, it becomes something else — a distorted or false love. Evil is one possibility when there is freedom or free will. If this were not so, then love would not be possible. Man and woman, who were created out of love, had to be made free in order for love to be real. This may explain why the possibility of evil (Satan's presence) in Paradise had to be allowed.

It is a great mystery why God allows evil in the world, but we must never forget that God is greater than any evil and can bring from it a greater good than we can imagine. We have the hope and confidence that one day, when Jesus returns, it will all be made clear to us and we will learn the full meaning of our human lives on this earth. For now, all we can do is use our free choice and choose God in everything we do. He is our true freedom. Our home is not this earth. Our home is in heaven with Him.

Dear Grace,

Why do Catholics say a prayer like the "Hail Mary" if it is not found in the Bible?

The Hail Mary, or *Ave Maria* (in Latin), is without a doubt one of the most beautiful and familiar prayers of the Universal Church. Your question asks why we recite this prayer if it is not found in the Bible. You may be surprised to learn, though, that actually the Hail Mary is very much rooted in Scripture. Let me say first, however, that prayer is, by definition, a call, cry, plea, or petition made to God. It does not necessarily have to be found explicitly in the Bible. Prayer is always a dialogue with God, and many of our most treasured prayers, including the Hail Mary, are assuredly inspired by or find their basis in Scripture.

The words of the Hail Mary are as follows: "Hail Mary, full of grace, the Lord is with thee; blessed art thou among women, and blessed is the fruit of thy womb, Jesus. Holy Mary, Mother of God, pray for us sinners, now and at the hour of our death. Amen." As may be easily recognized, the prayer can be said to have two parts, the first being a salutation, or greeting, and the second a petition, an earnest or urgent request.

Who was it that greeted Mary by saying, "Hail, full of grace, the Lord is with thee"? It was not a pope, a bishop, or church leader. It was the archangel Gabriel, the one who stands "in the presence of God" (Luke 1:19). Luke tells us the splendid and wondrous story of the Annunciation (see Luke 1:26-38). Although translations may vary, there can be no doubt that this first statement of greeting in the Hail Mary comes to us from the Gospel of Luke. Gabriel said these words, and he was a messenger sent directly from God. Thus, it is uncomplicated to see how the early Christians would adopt these beautiful words by the angel as soon as devotion to Mary sprang forth in the Church.

The second part of the greeting (which is the first half of the whole prayer) also comes from Scripture. Let us recall the words of Elizabeth when Mary visited her. When she heard Mary's greeting, Elizabeth, filled with the Holy Spirit, cried out in a loud voice, "Blessed are you among women, and blessed is the fruit of your womb!" (Luke 1:42). The Christians later added the name of Jesus in order to identify more exactly that He was the "fruit of Mary's womb." Thus, it is evident that the first half of the Hail Mary is taken directly from words found in the Bible, words spoken by the angel of the Lord and by Elizabeth, Mary's cousin, who also was chosen by God to give birth to John the Baptist, the one who would prepare the way for the Savior.

The Visitation account also leads us into the second half of the Hail Mary, which we said is a petition. The first thing we notice, though, is that this second half begins by declaring Mary to be holy. Again, we see in Luke's Gospel that the Blessed Virgin says this about herself in her Canticle (the *Magnificat*) — "henceforth all generations will call me blessed" (Luke 1:48). The word "blessed" and "holy" have the same meaning. Very interesting also in Luke's narrative is that he recounts Elizabeth as saying, "And why is this granted to me, that the mother of my Lord should come to me? . . . Blessed is she who believed that there would be a fulfilment of what was spoken to her from the Lord" (Luke 1:43-45). The Greek word for Lord is *Kyrios*, and this word is used many times in the New Testament to refer to God the Father (see Luke 1:6, 9, 11). There is substantial evidence, therefore, that the believers in Christ came to recognize Mary as the Mother of God. The Church, at the Council of Ephesus, later declared this officially in 431.

Finally, we come to the very last part, "pray for us sinners, now and at the hour of our death." Wanting to make the Hail Mary truly a prayer, a petition was eventually added, and thus it appeared in its completed form by the mid-sixteenth century. The Hail Mary is without question a very biblically rooted prayer, a salutation and petition to the Blessed Virgin, from whom the Redeemer of mankind was born. It is a prayer for all Christians.

Dear Grace,

Before and during the crucifixion, where was Joseph, the Virgin Mary's husband?

This question has indeed baffled countless people throughout the centuries, including some of the best Scripture scholars in the world. Based upon all of the writings we have, it is almost universally agreed upon that by the time Jesus began His public ministry Joseph had already died and, thus, would not have been present at the crucifixion.

Most of what we know of the life of Joseph comes to us from two of the four Gospels — those of Matthew and Luke — but they are for the most part silent about his death. The very last we hear of him is in Luke's account of the Finding in the Temple (see Luke 2:41-52). At this time, as we know, Jesus is twelve years old. Nothing more is said of Joseph except when Jesus is referred to as his son later in the Gospel (see John 1:45; 6:42; Luke 4:22; Matthew 13:55). For that matter, no more is said of Jesus' life from that moment until the beginning of His public ministry either. These are referred to as "the hidden years." One fact we clearly notice is that Joseph seems to no longer be present when the Gospel again takes up the life of Jesus at about the age of thirty.

The major reason that biblical scholars today agree on the probability that Joseph had already died by the time of Jesus' crucifixion comes from the narrative in the Gospel of John, which tells us that, from the cross, our Lord gave His Mother, Mary, to the beloved disciple John. We learn that "from that hour the disciple took her to his own home" (John 19:27). Why would Mary have been entrusted to John and taken into his home if her husband, Joseph, had still been living?

Another factor that supports the belief that Joseph had already died when Christ experienced His Passion and death is the fact that it has generally and consistently been accepted and believed that Joseph was much older than his wife, Mary, and therefore would have probably died much earlier than her. There is a possibility that this could be based on the details given about Joseph's life in other early writings, which, although not later included in the accepted canonical books of Scripture, had a wide circulation in the early years of the Church. These are known as the apocryphal (hidden) literature. Even though their trustworthiness and authenticity cannot by any means be totally relied upon, they do provide details that lend some support for what we believe regarding the death of Joseph occurring before the Passion of Christ.

While these writings carried no real authority, they nevertheless acquired in the course of ages some popularity. We can see that in them some of the truth was contained, but because the Church did not later accept them as inspired writings, some of the details found in them have to be questioned seriously. It could be that early Church writers were seeking answers to certain difficult biblical passages. Despite the fact that they are contrary to the tradition witnessed by old works of art, these writings have done much in retaining the belief that St. Joseph was an old man at the time of marriage with Mary, the Mother of God.

In the end, we must say that we do not know with any certainty when or where Joseph died. The important thing is to know that God chose him, a good and "just" man, for the very special mission and role of caring for and protecting the mother who was to bring forth the long-awaited Savior into the world. His marriage to the Blessed Mother was a holy and virginal one. He fulfilled his call from God faithfully, and therefore he deserves our honor, respect, and devotion.

4
Sacraments

Dear Grace,

My question is this: Where, when, and how did confession begin in the Catholic Church? I know non-Catholics often ridicule us for having to go to a priest to absolve our sins. I always answer that I have a feeling of peace once I have completed my confession, and that is why I do it. I am just wondering how it all began.

How wonderful that you feel this sense of peace after confession. This is the joy of reconciliation! Because of the shorter and shorter confession lines, it seems that many Catholics today do not have a clear understanding of the sacrament of Reconciliation, which is still most often referred to as "Confession." Why do Catholics "go to confession"? Quite simply, because Jesus told us to. When Jesus Christ walked on this earth, He knew that one day He would ascend to heaven when His mission was completed. He also knew that because our human nature has been wounded (not destroyed) by the original sin of the first man, Adam, we would always be in need of forgiveness from God for our offenses against Him. Yes, Baptism washes away original sin but not the tendency toward sin. If we have trouble understanding this tendency, all we must do is look at ourselves. Are we perfect? Are we not often drawn to do what is wrong? This is precisely why we have been given the sacrament of Reconciliation.

All of His life, Jesus offered mercy and forgiveness to a sinful humanity. He healed people and forgave them their sins, calling on them to "repent, and believe in the gospel" (Mark 1:15). Because

He established a Church on earth to carry on His work (with the guidance of the Holy Spirit), one of the main tasks of that Church, if she is to be true to Him, is to continue the reconciliation of sinners to God. How were we to obtain forgiveness of sins after Jesus returned to heaven? Why would He appoint men (the Apostles and their successors in the priesthood) to carry on this work? There are many who insist they do not need a priest. They believe that they can confess directly to God. But to say that is to ignore the specific instructions to the Apostles and to those who would take their place. There can be no mistake about the intentions of Jesus on this matter.

The sacrament of Reconciliation is referred to as Christ's Easter gift because that is exactly when He gave it to us. On that Sunday, the day of His glorious Resurrection, He appeared to His Apostles as they were gathered behind locked doors, afraid of what might happen to them if anyone knew they were followers of Jesus. He said to them, "Peace be with you. . . . As the Father has sent me, even so I send you. . . . Receive the Holy Spirit. If you forgive the sins of any, they are forgiven; if you retain the sins of any, they are retained" (John 20:19-23). Jesus wanted not only the people of His day to receive forgiveness of sins, but He also wanted all people throughout the ages to receive it. This was the purpose of His life. These are Jesus' words! He is the one who said we should do it this way!

It is true that priests are human beings and sinners themselves, as we all are, but Jesus Christ Himself, who was God, delegated to them the power to forgive sins *in His name*. When we confess our sins to a priest, we must remember that he stands there in place of Christ (*in Persona Christi*) and our forgiveness comes from Christ. Let us also not forget that, like every one of the seven sacraments given to us by Jesus, in the sacrament of Reconciliation, we receive grace, which leads to holiness. We have often forgotten that. So, we not only are forgiven, but we receive the gift of God's grace, a special help to turn away from sin in the future. God, who made each and every one of us, knows exactly what we need. Can anyone afford to turn down this free gift from Him? If we were to receive it more often, we would experience a peace and joy unlike any that we have ever known.

Dear Grace,

Can you tell me what is the official list of questions that the priest is required to ask in the confessional?

In answer to your question, there is no "official list" of questions that a priest must ask. Canon law states that in posing questions, the priest must "proceed with prudence and discretion." When it is necessary, he is to help us to make a complete confession. This would be especially true when the person has not been to confession for a number of years. He is to urge the penitent to repent sincerely of his or her offenses against God. Sometimes this means asking certain general questions in order to ascertain whether the sins are mortal or venial and also to see if the person is truly sorry for these sins. The priest is there to help us. He is happy that we are there, seeking reconciliation with God! When and if he asks us questions, it is only so that he will be better able to administer the sacrament to us and guide us on the path to holiness.

Dear Grace,

Why may non-Catholics not receive Communion at a Catholic Mass?

This is a question that is not easy to answer, mainly because many view the Church as made up of so many rules. However, when we look at Scripture and Tradition, we see that the Catholic Church teaches what she believes has come to her from God. As Catholics, we believe that the Church is "one." In other words, when Jesus left this earth in bodily form, He did not leave many churches; He left one Church. He also left for us the seven sacraments, to be administered by the Church. Of these, the Eucharist is the sacrament of sacraments and our surest and most clear sign of unity.

The Eucharist is our expression of faith in everything that Jesus taught us. At the Mass, we try to do as He asked us. He said, "This is my body. . . . This is my blood. . . . Do this in remembrance of me" (Matthew 26:26, 28; Luke 22:19). Catholics believe that at the consecration of the gifts of bread and wine, they are supernaturally transformed into the Body and Blood of Jesus Christ Himself. We have His Real Presence. When we eat His body and drink His blood as He told us to, then we, although many, become one Body in Christ. This is Holy Communion.

When Catholics receive and share Holy Communion, we respond by saying a firm "Amen." By this, we mean "I believe." We believe in everything that the one, holy, catholic, and apostolic Church teaches. Therefore, the Eucharist, or Holy Communion, is to be received only by those who are "in full communion" with the Catholic Church and her teachings. There are certain exceptions to this, but generally speaking, why would someone want to partake of something half way? Holy Communion is an "either all or nothing" kind of thing. It is the constant prayer of the Catholic Church (and should be of every Catholic) that one day all Christians may be united at the table of the Lord. Then Jesus' prayer "that they may be one" (John 17:11) will be fulfilled and then how pleased God will be. To some this sounds impossible, but with God all things are possible.

Dear Grace,

Does a person have to be dying to receive the sacrament of Anointing of the Sick? What ever happened to "extreme unction"?

No, the Anointing of the Sick is no longer considered to be a sacrament only for those who are in danger of death. This change in understanding came about when the Second Vatican Council restored the sacrament to its original purpose and meaning. St. James, presumably a cousin of Christ, gives us a clear example of how the sacrament was celebrated in the early Church: "Is any among you sick? Let him call for the elders of the church, and let them pray over him, anointing him with oil in the name of the Lord; and the prayer of faith will save the sick man, and the Lord will raise him up; and if he has committed sins, he will be forgiven" (James 5:14-15). The forgiveness of sins meant that grace was bestowed on the person. Thus, the anointing was a sacrament.

The name "extreme unction" did not even come into use until the end of the twelfth century. The word "unction" means "anointing." This unction was regarded as the last in the order of the sacramental unctions, and it probably was intended to mean "the anointing of the dying." In other words, over a period of time, the purpose and meaning shifted from the way it was originally intended. Catholics today facing death, serious illness, or even the trials of old age should receive this sacrament. It is also certainly fitting to receive Anointing of the Sick just before a serious surgery and, even if the person recovers his health and then later becomes ill again, he or she may be anointed again. The sacrament gives us the strength we need to endure whatever suffering lies ahead.

The moment that a person begins to be in danger of death, a priest should be called immediately. Priests will attempt to do their best to rush to the side of a dying person because a person's salvation could be at stake. Satan would like nothing better than to snatch a person right at the moment of death. This is why the Church responds quickly when the sacrament of Anointing of the Sick is requested. One more thing to remember is that there is one "last" sacrament before death, and that is Holy Communion. This is called "Viaticum" — a Latin term meaning "provisions for the journey." In this case, the Eucharist is the sacrament of passing over from this world to the Father. It is when Confession, Anointing, and Viaticum are administered together that we might refer to it as the "Last Rites," although this term is rarely used today.

Dear Grace,

I have a problem and need your help. I am ashamed to say that I have forgotten how to go to confession and I know that it is time for me to go. Maybe if you explained the steps to me, it would help other people also.

I think it is wonderful that you wish to be reconciled to God. I am happy to help you. Confession is not difficult, but it does require preparation. We need to review our lives since our last confession and search our thoughts, words, and actions to see in what ways we have offended God's love, His law, and the laws of the Church, especially those sins that we have committed with full knowledge and full consent. This is called an examination of conscience.

The following are the basic steps in the sacrament of Reconciliation: Begin your confession by making the sign of the cross and greeting the priest in the following manner: "Bless me Father, for I have sinned." The priest gives you a blessing and you respond, "Lord, you know all things; you know I love you." You then continue, "My last confession was...."

Confess all your sins to the priest. He will help you make a good confession. If you are unsure about how to confess or you feel uneasy, just ask him to help you. Answer his questions without hiding or holding back anything out of fear or shame. Place your trust in God, a merciful Father who wants to forgive you. Following your confession of sins, say the following: "I am sorry for these and all my sins." The priest will assign you a penance and offer advice to help you on your spiritual journey. You will then recite an Act of Contrition, expressing sorrow for your sins. The priest, acting in the person of Christ, will then absolve you of your sins and you may go. What a wonderful feeling it is to be reconciled with God.

Dear Grace,

Why is it that the Catholic Church baptizes infants when they are not yet able to speak for themselves and choose the faith they wish to be a part of? Is this practice found in the Bible?

Yes, the Church's practice of baptizing infants is indeed very biblical. First of all, we know that Jesus said very clearly that "unless one is born of water and the Spirit, he cannot enter the kingdom of God" (John 3:5). He was speaking of Baptism and its necessity for salvation. Now, why would He leave out infants when He also said, "Let the children come to me, and do not hinder them; for to such belongs the kingdom of heaven" (Matthew 19:14)?

Jesus established a New Covenant, and the sign for entering was Baptism. We have the biblical witness that in the very early Church entire households were baptized. Certainly they would not have left out their children! In fact, after the Holy Spirit came upon the Apostles at Pentecost, Peter began to preach the Good News of Jesus Christ and when he was asked what was required to enter, he said the following, "Repent, and be baptized every one of you in the name of Jesus Christ for the forgiveness of your sins; and you shall receive the gift of the Holy Spirit. For the promise is to you and to your *children* and to all that are far off, every one whom the Lord our God calls to him" (Acts 2:38-39; emphasis added).

Dear Grace,

I have not been to confession in a very long time and there is something I would like to know. A friend told me that, under certain conditions, a priest could divulge what you tell him, even in confession. Is this true?

Your friend is wrong. I have heard this question before, and it is a shame how misinformation can keep a person from receiving the healing that Jesus offers us in the sacrament of Reconciliation — better known to many as "Confession." The Catholic Church asserts "that every priest who hears confessions is bound under very severe penalties to keep absolute secrecy regarding the sins that his penitents have confessed to him. He can make no use of knowledge that confession gives him about penitents' lives [cf. CIC, can. 1388 § 1; CCEO, can. 1456]. This secret, which admits of no exceptions, is called the 'sacramental seal,' because what the penitent has made known to the priest remains 'sealed' by the sacrament" (CCC, n. 1467).

A priest can speak to no one of anything you say to him in confession, and this includes you. For example, even if he is aware of your identity, and later runs into you in church or elsewhere, he may not bring up anything you said to him in confession, unless you first bring it up to him. Then, and only then, may he discuss it with you. Otherwise, he must remain silent. Under no circumstances may the "seal" of confession be broken. According to canons 983 and 1388 of the Code of Canon Law, the penalty for a priest who violates this seal would be an automatic excommunication, reserved to the Apostolic See.

It is very important to understand that when we confess our sins before a priest, he is standing there *in Persona Christi* (in the Person of Christ). It is Christ Himself who hears our confession and forgives us. Jesus gave us this sacrament because He knew that we would continue to sin and be in need of reconciliation with God. So, He gave to His Apostles the authority to forgive sins "in His name" when He said to them, "Whatever you bind on earth shall be bound in heaven, and whatever you loose on earth shall be loosed in heaven" (Matthew 16:19).

When we stay away from confession, it is for a number of reasons. Sometimes, it is shame over what we have done. Or perhaps we think that the priest is going to be shocked by what we will say. I can assure you, however, that he will be happy that we are there, seeking reconciliation with God. Sin offends God, but He is always ready to forgive, if we will only turn to Him and ask. Do not put it off any longer; go as soon as you can. You will experience a joy and peace that the world can never offer. God loves you so much and His mercy is far greater than you may realize.

Listen to the words of Jesus as spoken to St. Maria Faustina Kowalska and recorded in her diary: "I want to give myself to souls and to fill them with My love, but few there are who want to accept all the graces My love has intended for them [p. 388]. Speak to the world about My mercy; let all mankind recognize My unfathomable mercy [p. 333]. The flames of mercy are burning Me — clamoring to be spent; I want to keep pouring them out to souls; souls just don't want to believe in My goodness [p. 99]. I desire trust from My creatures. Encourage souls to place great trust in My fathomless mercy. Let the weak, sinful soul have no fear to approach Me, for even if it had more sins than there are grains of sand in the world, all would be drowned in the immeasurable depths of My mercy [p. 400]" (*Diary: Divine Mercy in My Soul*).

Dear Grace,

I know that I am supposed to fast for one hour before receiving Communion, but I am confused about something. Is this fast to be one hour before the beginning of Mass or one hour before the actual receiving of Communion?

Canon 919 states that "one who is to receive the Most Holy Eucharist is to abstain from any food or drink, with the exception only of water and medicine, for at least the period of one hour before Holy Communion." As you can see, the Eucharistic fast is to be one hour from Communion, not the time that Mass begins. Customarily, the priest who says the Mass must fast one hour from the time Mass begins. Your fast, however, must be such that you do not eat within one hour of Communion.

You might recall that the required fast used to be much longer. It was later shortened to allow more persons to receive Communion. The idea here is not that it is sinful to mix the food in our bodies with the Body of Christ, but rather to show reverence for the Real Presence of Christ in the Holy Eucharist. Thus, if a person is unsure if it has been one hour, he does not have to allow this to prevent him or her from receiving Communion. Every reasonable effort should be made, however, to observe the fast. The fast, by the way, is not binding on the aged, the infirm, or their caretakers.

Dear Grace,

Some of my friends have questioned me about why and how I can believe that Jesus Christ is truly present in the Host, which we receive at Communion in Mass. Sometimes I am not sure

exactly how to explain it well enough so that it will be understood. Can you help me with this?

The answer to this question will require a lengthy response. It is true that many people consider the Catholic Church's beliefs about the Eucharist to be totally unbelievable and almost outrageous. Catholics actually believe that when a priest, during the Holy Sacrifice of the Mass, repeats the words of Jesus at the Last Supper over the bread and wine, they become the real Body and Blood of the Lord Himself. How can this be? Where did the Church get this idea? We believe it because Jesus said it, and this Word of His is transmitted to us in various ways.

One of these ways is precisely the one that many Catholics are challenged on today — the Bible. In addition to the testimony of the Sacred Scriptures, however, we also have Sacred Tradition — that which the Apostles handed down to us and which they learned from Christ. We also have the teaching of the Church, given the authority to teach by Jesus in His name. Let us look first, then, at the Bible to see how exactly the Church can so confidently teach what she does.

It is evident in the Gospel of John that, very early in His ministry, Jesus gave the first promise of the Eucharist (see John 6). A crowd of five thousand had just witnessed one of Christ's greatest miracles (the multiplication of the loaves) and they were in great awe at what they had experienced. So, they follow Him to Capernaum, wanting Him to perform more signs. When they begin to speak about the manna that God gave to their ancestors to eat in the desert, Jesus uses this opportunity to give a discourse that every Christian should read and reread very carefully.

"I am the bread of life," He said (John 6:35). "I am the living bread which came down from heaven; if any one eats of this bread, he will live for ever; and the bread which I shall give for the life of the world is my flesh" (John 6:51). The Scripture then says that this shocked the Jews. How could he give them His flesh to eat? He answered by saying, "Unless you eat the flesh of the Son of man and drink his blood, you have no life in you; he who eats my flesh and drinks my blood has eternal life, and I will raise him up at the last day. For my flesh is food indeed, and my blood is drink indeed. He who eats my flesh and drinks my blood abides in me, and I in him" (John 6:53-56). These were very powerful words, and they are the words of Jesus Christ. He was telling them that the bread that He would give for the life of the world was His flesh!

At this point, many of them left His company, but we notice that Jesus did not call them back saying, "I didn't mean it the way you think I did." This is because He did mean it! If Jesus had meant His words to be taken symbolically only, then He would have had to explain this to His disciples, but He does not. This is very important. Now, He thought the rest of them would leave also, but then Peter responds by giving one of the most moving answers in all human history. "Lord, to whom shall we go? You have the words of eternal life" (John 6:68). At that moment, Peter may not have even realized the full import of what he was declaring, but later it would become clear to him.

In verse 47 of John 6, Jesus states, "He who believes has eternal life." What was He talking about? It must have been the teaching that He was giving them. Over and over in these passages He repeats and reaffirms that He is the Bread of Life and that "if any one eats of this bread, he will live for ever" and the bread He will give for the life of the world "is my flesh" (John 6:51). It takes great faith to accept and believe these words of our Lord, but we should never allow our predispositions or traditions to restrict us from recognizing the truth that Jesus wished to teach us. Our Lord said, "Blessed are those who have not seen and yet believe" (John 20:29).

The Catholic Church teaches that God's Revelation is transmitted to us not only through Sacred Scripture but also by Sacred Tradition and that these are interpreted by the authoritative and authentic teaching of the Church — the Magisterium. First, we have looked at the testimony regarding the Real Presence of Jesus in the Holy Eucharist found in the Bible, and we read Jesus' own words. Now we want to ask what it is that we learn from Tradition regarding the Church's teaching on the Eucharist.

When we speak of Tradition with a capital "T" we are referring to what has been handed down to us by the Apostles and their followers, in both oral and written form. The earliest written account of belief by the early Church in the presence of Jesus in the Holy Eucharist comes from the First Letter of Paul to the Corinthians, chapter 11, verses 23, 24, and 26. He says, "For I received from the Lord what I also delivered to you, that the Lord Jesus on the night he was betrayed took bread, and when he had given thanks, he broke it, and said, 'This is my body which is for you. Do this in remembrance of me.' . . . For as often as you eat this bread and drink the cup, you proclaim the Lord's death until he comes."

It is believed by some scholars that this account of the celebration of the Lord's Last Supper was written approximately fifty-seven years after Christ. In another verse from that same chapter, Paul states, "Whoever, therefore, eats the bread or drinks the cup of the Lord in an unworthy manner will be guilty of profaning the body and blood of the Lord" (1 Corinthians 11:27). This clearly indicates that the early Christians truly believed that the Eucharist was indeed the Body and Blood of Jesus. In 350, St. Cyril of Jerusalem wrote about this passage and stated, "Since Christ himself has declared the bread to be his body, who can have any further doubt? Since he himself has said quite categorically, *This is my blood*, who would dare to question and say that it is not his blood? Therefore, it is with complete assurance that we receive the bread and wine as the body and blood of Christ" (*Catecheses*).

There is an enormous amount of historical evidence in the writings of the early Church Fathers that testifies to belief in the Real Presence. These men were prominent writers of the early Church whose works manifested a pronounced theological sophistication. Why should this be important for us today? It matters because some of them received what they taught firsthand from the Apostles. And the Apostles learned it directly from Jesus Himself. He gave to them the authority to teach in His name. He even said, "He who hears you hears me" (Luke 10:16).

St. Ignatius of Antioch, writing in the year 110, bears a strong witness when he expresses the following: "I have no taste for corruptible food nor for the pleasures of this life. I desire the bread of God, which is the flesh of Jesus Christ, who was of the seed of David; and for drink I desire his blood, which is love incorruptible" (*Letter to the Romans*, 7, 3). These are powerful words! And it is only one example of the numerous early writings regarding the Holy Eucharist. This is Sacred Tradition.

The Catholic Church has consistently taught belief in the Real Presence from the very beginning to the present day. In the first thousand years, Christians generally did not deny it, although there were some heresies. It was not until the Protestant Reformation, fifteen centuries after Christ's death, that rejection of the Real Presence gained a following of any significance.

Jesus knew how we would hunger for this "food," which is Him, and He provided ways for us to know that it is available to us. He revealed it through Sacred Scripture and Sacred Tradition, and these are interpreted and taught by the Church.

Dear Grace,

What does the Catholic Church teach about what happens to children who die without being baptized? Do they go to heaven or hell? What ever happened to the teaching about limbo?

Jesus taught clearly that "unless one is born of water and the Spirit, he cannot enter the kingdom of God" (John 3:5). He was speaking of Baptism and its necessity for salvation. We understand Him to mean that there were no exceptions to this requirement, and this cannot be taken lightly. Every word that He uttered was for our good and our salvation. Throughout the ages, this teaching of Christ has left His followers wondering what happens to those who die without being baptized, especially innocent children.

Every man, woman, and child is born into this world with a fallen human nature that is tainted by original sin. We are not guilty of that sin, but we have inherited its consequences. Anyone who doubts this must simply look at himself or herself. If we do that, we see the effects of that sin in our lives and behavior. Look at how we are drawn to do that which is wrong, sometimes even when we do not want to. Because of this, children, as well as adults, are in need of the cleansing sacrament of Baptism. Through it "we are freed from sin and reborn as sons of God" (CCC, n. 1213).

If Baptism is necessary for salvation, then what does the Church teach happens to those who die without it? The Church has been entrusted by Christ to proclaim the Gospel to all nations and to have them baptized. We thus understand Baptism to be necessary for those who have heard the Gospel and who have had the possibility of asking for this sacrament. Scripture makes clear to us that God "wants all men to be saved" (1 Timothy 2:4). Therefore, we believe and teach that "every man who is ignorant of the Gospel of Christ and of his Church, but seeks the truth and does the will of God in accordance with his understanding of it, can be saved" (CCC, n. 1260).

This, of course, does not mean that we should go along through life thinking that it does not matter what we do because in the end God is going to save us. Remember that there will be an accounting for everything we have done in this life and each will receive his or her due reward or justice. The Lord sees all our thoughts and actions. Yes, He loves us and wants us to lead a happy life, and the best way to have that is to be close to Him always. We must ever be working on our salvation and the salvation of the world, especially those we love most — our families and children.

Infants are not guilty of any personal sin because they have not yet reached the age of reason, but they are born with the stain of original sin. This is why it is very important that they be baptized as soon as possible after their birth. The Catholic Church has never formally taught belief in a state of "limbo" for infants dying without Baptism. Certain theologians in the past suggested that there might exist a state in which these infants would live a life of eternal bliss, but excluded from heaven.

What we do believe is the following: "As regards *children who have died without Baptism*, the Church can only entrust them to the mercy of God, as she does in her funeral rites for them. Indeed, the great mercy of God who desires that all men should be saved, and Jesus' tenderness toward children which caused him to say: 'Let the children come to me, do not hinder them' [*Mk* 10:14; cf. *1 Tim* 2:4], allow us to hope that there is a way of salvation for children who have died without Baptism. All the more urgent is the Church's call not to prevent little children [from] coming to Christ through the gift of holy Baptism" (CCC, n. 1261).

Dear Grace,

I have a relative who was married in the Catholic Church. She never had her three children baptized and they are now full grown and totally lost with no faith or a church. The parent wanted the children to decide on a religion when they grew up. Who will be held accountable by God for this, the parent or the children who are now grown up?

In a case like this, the parent is held to be responsible first. The grown children become also accountable, however, after hearing the Gospel of Jesus Christ and having had the possibility of asking for this sacrament (see CCC, n. 1257). Before ascending to heaven, Jesus commanded His Apostles, "Go into all the world and preach the gospel to the whole creation. He who believes and is baptized will be saved; but he who does not believe will be condemned" (Mark 16:15-16). In other words, if the children have learned about Jesus Christ and have had an opportunity to ask to be baptized, then they are now responsible. It becomes a matter between them and God. We have to believe this because of what Jesus said. In addition, the parent will also be accountable for any part she played. Nothing goes unnoticed by God.

You say that your relative was married in the Catholic Church. If she was Catholic, then in her preparation for marriage, she had to make a sincere promise to do all in her power to have all of her children baptized and brought up in the Catholic faith (see canon 1125). It is a serious matter to make this promise to God and then ignore it or decide otherwise. All human persons come into this world with a fallen human nature that is wounded by original sin. Every infant, therefore, is in need of Baptism to be freed from it. A believing parent would be denying this to her own child if she did not have him baptized shortly after birth (see CCC, n. 1250).

Dear Grace,

My brother's ex-wife belongs to another religion. Their daughter is not baptized in the Catholic Church. Is there anything that we as a family can do to get this done? Do both parents have to consent?

The answer depends on the particular situation. First, has the child already been baptized in her mother's religion? If so, then you would need to find out how it was done. The Catholic Church believes in only one Baptism for the forgiveness of sins. The requirement is that it must have been celebrated using the baptismal formula that Jesus gave — "in the name of the Father and of the Son and of the Holy Spirit" (Matthew 28:19) — and there must also have been immersion, pouring, or sprinkling of water. If this was done, then that Baptism is valid, and for life.

If the child, however, has never been baptized but is living in the legal custody of a parent practicing another religion, there may be nothing you can do for now except to pray and be an example, taking the child to Mass when she is with you and teaching her about Christ, so that one day she may seek Baptism for herself. The reason for this is that the Church believes Baptism to be the entrance into a new life in Christ. If there is no hope that the child will be brought up in the Catholic faith, then the Baptism is to be put off. In danger of death, however, the child is licitly baptized, even against the will of the parents (see canon 868).

Dear Grace,

I would like to know if you could please find out if we as grandparents can baptize our grandson. Is this allowed under

Church rules? Both my wife and I are Catholics and so are our grandson's parents.

The way your question is asked implies that you yourselves desire to baptize your grandson. In the Catholic Church, the ordinary minister of Baptism is a bishop, priest, or deacon (see canon 861). Only in an emergency could another person baptize, as long as the person used the trinitarian baptismal formula ("I baptize you in the name of the Father, and of the Son, and of the Holy Spirit"). The person who baptizes someone in case of necessity or emergency must also have the required intention; they must "will to do what the Church does when she baptizes" (CCC, n. 1256).

Many Catholics do not realize that they can baptize someone in an emergency situation. It is, however, our Christian responsibility and duty. Jesus Himself said that Baptism is necessary for salvation (see John 3:5). Therefore, if we ever found ourselves in a situation where, for example, a person was in danger of death, one of the first thoughts to come to our mind should be for that person's salvation. We would immediately ask him if he has ever been baptized. If the answer is no, but the person expresses that he would like to be baptized, then we would take water and, while we recite the trinitarian formula, sprinkle, pour, or immerse him with or in the water. That person would then be baptized. One should see to it also that the Baptism is properly recorded by informing the pastor of the parish in which the Baptism was conferred (see canon 878).

Reading your question carefully, I also wonder if perhaps you are asking if you as grandparents can be the sponsors for your grandson's Baptism. If this is what you mean, then there appears to be nothing to prevent you. Canon law merely specifies that the sponsor(s) not be the father or mother of the one to be baptized (see canon 874, para. 1, n. 5). You, of course, have to have been confirmed and have received Holy Communion, in addition to leading a life in harmony with the faith and the role you are undertaking as sponsors. It will be up to you to assist the parents in helping your grandson to live the Christian life, which begins with Baptism, and to fulfill faithfully the obligations connected with it. What a privilege and honor that is!

Dear Grace,

If you are not "confirmed," does that mean your soul is lost and you will not go to heaven?

No, you will certainly not go to hell if you are not confirmed. By not receiving the sacrament of Confirmation, however, you will be missing out on one of the greatest graces that Christ gives us in order to get to heaven, namely the full outpouring of the Holy Spirit. The *Catechism of the Catholic Church* (n. 1306) states the following: "Every baptized person not yet confirmed can and should receive the sacrament of Confirmation [cf. CIC, can. 889 § 1]. Since Baptism, Confirmation, and Eucharist form a unity, it follows that 'the faithful are obliged to receive this sacrament at the appropriate time' [CIC, can. 890], for without Confirmation and Eucharist, Baptism is certainly valid and efficacious, but Christian initiation remains incomplete." If it is true that Baptism is still valid and we are saved even without Confirmation, then why do we need it and why did Jesus give it to us?

The Catholic Church believes and teaches that Jesus instituted seven sacraments, or "signs," of the bestowal of God's grace. He knew that after His mission on earth was complete and He returned to the Father, our nature — which has been wounded by original sin — would continue to be in need of grace in order that we might attain our destiny, which is heaven. Thus, every time we receive a sacrament, we receive grace, that undeserved gift, or "help," from God. On our own, we are too weak and limited to make it to heaven. It is always and only with God's help that we do so. The sacraments are the "channels," if you will, by which God gives us this grace that we are so badly in need of. A sacrament is a "sign" like no other sign because it makes what it points to become real for us. Through it and because of it, we encounter Christ, and our faith is strengthened.

The evidence of Jesus' intention regarding Confirmation is clear in the Scriptures. The Book of Acts records that fifty days after the first Easter Sunday, the Apostles were gathered in hiding in the upper room in the city of Jerusalem. The Lord Himself, before ascending to heaven, had told them to wait there. "Suddenly a sound came from heaven like the rush of a mighty wind, and it filled all the house where they were sitting. And there appeared to them tongues as of fire, distributed and resting on each one of them. And they were all filled with the Holy Spirit and began to speak in other tongues, as the Spirit gave them utterance" (Acts 2:1-4).

So, it was on that first Pentecost Sunday that the Holy Spirit came upon the Apostles in a most powerful way. In fact, it was so powerful that something supernatural happened. They began to speak in languages they did not know! This was their "confirmation" of the presence of the Holy Spirit. Now, all the fear they had felt left them. Peter, who had just a few weeks before denied Jesus three times out of fear, stood up and gave one of the most bold and convincing speeches in Christian history. The Bible tells us that three thousand people were converted to Christ that very day (see Acts 2:41).

Scripture also reveals for us that after Philip, the deacon, had baptized a large number of people in Samaria, Peter and John "came down and prayed for them that they might receive the Holy Spirit; for it had not yet fallen on any of them, but they had only been baptized in the name of the Lord Jesus. Then they laid their hands on them and they received the Holy Spirit" (Acts 8:14-17). Even though the Bible does not use the word "confirmation," it appears that the Baptism those in Samaria had received was now made complete by the coming of the Holy Spirit after the "laying on of hands." They were now "confirmed" and received supernatural strength to fight the battle that lies ahead always for every Christian.

Without the confirmation of the Holy Spirit, Peter and the Apostles would never have had the courage or strength to go out into the world and spread the Good News of Jesus Christ. It is the same for us today. Living in the world in which we do, can we as Christians afford to turn down this powerful gift from God? When we are baptized, our parents or we make the decision to take up the "good fight." At Confirmation, we receive our armor (strength) for the battle, and at the Eucharist, we receive the "food" for the journey. These are the three sacraments of initiation. We need all three in order to enter fully into the Christian life. And even though not being confirmed does not mean we will go to hell, we need it so that we will be sure we have all the help necessary to get to heaven.

Dear Grace,

I have a question after reading about the Virgin of Guadalupe. It states that, by a special order from the bishop, Juan Diego could receive Holy Communion three times a week. My question is: How often can you receive Holy Communion — once a day, twice a day, more than twice, or just once a week?

It is true that in the year 1531, after the "miracle of the roses" — which confirmed the appearance of the Blessed Virgin Mother of God at Tepeyac Hill in New Spain (later known as Mexico) — Bishop Don Juan de Zumarraga granted to Juan Diego a very special permission to receive Holy Communion three days a week at Mass. In the sixteenth century, this was an unusual accommodation. The reason that it was so unusual at that time was due to a historical rigorism similar to Jansenism, a movement that, in the seventeenth century, became widespread in France and the Spanish Netherlands. Essentially, the idea was that human nature was so corrupted by original sin that only the "elect" could be saved. They had such a deep sense of unworthiness, and this caused them to be strongly opposed to frequent Communion. People did not feel good enough to approach the table of the Lord.

The Council of Trent attempted to refute this by reinforcing the Church's original understanding of frequent Communion when it declared: "At each Mass the faithful who are present should communicate [receive Communion], not only in spiritual desire, but sacramentally, by the actual reception of the Eucharist" (Session 22, Chap. 6). It was the definitive wish of the Church that all Christians should be daily nourished by this heavenly banquet and should derive therefore more abundant fruit for their sanctification. But the rigoristic view of considering people unworthy of daily Communion continued long after the sixteenth century.

In 1905, the Catholic Church addressed this issue again in the Decree on the Frequent and Daily Reception of Holy Communion (*Sacra Tridentina*). The document makes clear that it was Jesus Himself, more than once, and in clarity of word, who pointed out the necessity of frequently eating His flesh and drinking His blood, especially in these words: "This is the bread which came down from heaven, not such as the fathers ate and died; he who eats this bread will live for ever" (John 6:58).

As *Sacra Tridentina* further explains, the idea of frequent Communion "had been understood clearly by the early Christians and they daily hastened to this table of life and strength. They continued steadfastly in the teaching of the Apostles and in the communion of the breaking of the bread (Acts 2:42). Piety, however, grew cold, and especially afterward because of the widespread plague of Jansenism, disputes began to arise concerning the dispositions with which one ought to receive frequent and daily Communion. Writers vied with one another demanding more and more stringent conditions as necessary to be fulfilled. The result of such disputes was that very few were considered worthy to receive the Holy Eucharist daily, and to derive from this most health-giving sacrament its more abundant fruits; the others were content to partake of it once a year, or once a month, or at most once a week. To such a degree, indeed, was this rigorism carried that whole classes of persons were excluded from a frequent approach to the holy table."

This was the thinking during the sixteenth century in which Juan Diego lived. Today, however, Catholics are allowed and encouraged to receive Holy Communion every day. Under very specific circumstances, it may even be permitted to receive twice a day.

Dear Grace,

What are the benefits of receiving frequent Communion?

In the sixteenth century and thereafter, many Catholics were discouraged from receiving Holy Communion frequently, due to the universal belief of human unworthiness taught by a widespread historical rigorism. Let us look at what the Catholic Church teaches about this. The Code of Canon Law reads as follows: "A person who has received the Most Holy Eucharist may receive it again on the same day only during the celebration of the Eucharist in which the person participates" (canon 917). It also stipulates that "even if they have received Communion in the same day, those who are in danger of death are strongly urged to receive again" (canon 921, para. 2).

The Church permits receiving twice in one day in order to allow for those situations when, for unusual circumstances, a person attends more than one Eucharistic celebration in the same day. There are several situations when this would apply. For example, it would occur when one must attend a funeral Mass or a wedding Mass after having received Communion already that day.

We see, then, that ecclesiastical discipline restricts the reception of Communion to once a day. Many Catholics, however, do not receive it even once a day. One might easily wonder why this is so. All Catholics, after they have been initiated into the Most Holy Eucharist, are bound by the obligation of receiving Communion at least once a year, and it must be fulfilled during the Easter season unless it is fulfilled for a just cause at some other time during the year (see canon 920, para. 2). Consider these words of Jesus: "Truly, truly, I say to you, unless you eat the flesh of the Son of man and drink his blood, you have no life in you; he who eats my flesh and drinks my blood has eternal life, and I will raise him up at the last day. For my flesh is food indeed, and my blood is drink indeed. He who eats my flesh and drinks my blood abides in me, and I in him" (John 6:53-56).

In other words, to receive the Eucharist is to receive Jesus the Lord Himself! If we, who love Him so, could see Him with our own eyes, would we say to Him, "Come back in one year and I will receive you again"? Of course not. We would want Him every day! And this is not only because we love Him but also because we need Him. Without Him, we are lost. We need this "food and drink" in order to live! After all, He said that without it we would have no life.

What does receiving Holy Communion do for us? What are the fruits? What does it result in? The *Catechism of the Catholic Church* explains it very clearly in paragraphs 1391 through 1401. The principal fruit of receiving Holy Communion is that it brings about an intimate union with Christ. This is the most important result, but in addition to this, receiving Jesus also helps to separate us from sin. Many Catholics, for example, do not realize that. During the Penitential Rite when the priest says, "Let us call to mind our sins," the faithful may confess their venial sins to God and then be prepared to receive Him bodily. The venial sins confessed during the rite are wiped away by the power of the Eucharist. Holy Communion also strengthens us to fight off the temptation toward sin. The more we unite ourselves to Christ, the less we will be drawn to sin.

Finally, Communion results in a deeper sense of union among all the faithful, the Church — the Mystical Body of Christ. As St. Paul writes, "Because there is one bread, we who are many are one body, for we all partake of the one bread" (1 Corinthians 10:17). When we enter the church for Mass, we are many people, but after Communion, we become one Body. Being aware of all this and knowing that we may receive Jesus in the flesh once a year or once a day, what will we choose?

Dear Grace,

Why is it that drinking of the wine (blood of Christ) is not mandatory during the Eucharist? I am in my fifties and a lifelong Catholic who attends Mass every Sunday and I do not understand why this has never been made mandatory. I have been attending

the same parish and there were times when the Precious Blood was not even offered to the general congregation. I am concerned about this, since in the Gospels Jesus says that one cannot enter the kingdom of heaven unless one eats his body and drinks his blood.

Yes, it is true that in John 6:53-54, Jesus declares, "Truly, truly, I say to you, unless you eat the flesh of the Son of man and drink his blood, you have no life in you; he who eats my flesh and drinks my blood has eternal life, and I will raise him up at the last day." Notice, however, that just a few lines down Jesus also states the following: "This is the bread which came down from heaven, not such as the fathers ate and died; he who eats this bread will live for ever" (John 6:58). He mentions only the bread (His body) in this verse. The Church came to understand this to mean that Jesus may be received totally and completely under both forms of bread and wine. Otherwise, the Body and Blood of Christ would be divided.

It is historically evident, from the writings of the early Church Fathers, that it was firmly believed that Christ was truly present in every particle of the body, or bread, and every drop of the blood, or wine. For example, Cyril of Jerusalem, writing in the mid-fourth century, warned the faithful to be extremely careful so that not even "a crumb, more precious than gold or jewels" would fall from their hands to the ground (see *Catecheses*, V, n. 21). His *Catecheses* reveals that Communion under both forms of bread and wine was practiced in the early Church. We also know that later, because of the challenge of the Reformers, the Church was led to officially declare her teaching that Jesus is present totally in both species.

Responding to the Reformers, the Council of Trent taught that there is no divine precept binding the laity or noncelebrating priests to receive the sacrament under both kinds (see Trent, Session 21, canon 1). By reason of the hypostatic union and of the indivisibility of His glorified humanity, Christ is really present and is received whole and entire, Body and Blood, Soul and Divinity, under either species alone. In addition, as regards the fruits of the sacrament, the Council clarified that the person who receives Communion under one kind is not deprived of any grace necessary for salvation (see Trent, Session 21, canon 3).

The new 2000 edition of the *General Instruction of the Roman Missal* states the following: "Moved by the same spirit and pastoral concern, the Second Vatican Council was able to reevaluate the Tridentine norm on communion under both kinds. No one today challenges the doctrinal principals on the completeness of Eucharistic communion under the form of bread alone. The Council thus gave permission for the reception of communion under both kinds on some occasions, because this more explicit form of the sacramental sign offers a special means of deepening the understanding of the mystery in which the faithful are taking part" (n. 14). So, we see that Communion under both kinds is allowed on some occasions, but it is definitely not required, as Christ is completely present under either form of bread or wine alone.

Dear Grace,

I had a miscarriage after three and a half months of pregnancy. I have read that in order to go to heaven, you need to be baptized. Am I correct in thinking that my baby went to heaven even if he didn't have a chance to get baptized?

Your concern for your baby's salvation is so moving and truly demonstrates your loving, maternal care. The Church also, as a mother, watches over her children and wishes that all might arrive at that heavenly bliss with her Lord. Your question is unusual in that it seeks an answer regarding Baptism and the attainment of heaven for an unborn child. Although the Church cannot pronounce with absolute certainty on the actual resting place of an unborn child who dies before birth, we most certainly have every reason to believe that the unborn do indeed go to be with God. There are numerous biblical passages that speak of the love and care that God has for every unborn child and these fill us with hope that, in His divine plan, He will always make a way for all unborn children to return to Him.

The mystery of life in the unborn is eloquently addressed by our Holy Father John Paul II in his inspiring and impassioned encyclical *Evangelium Vitae* ("The Gospel of Life"). There, he states the following: "Human life is sacred and inviolable at every moment of existence, including the initial phase which precedes birth. All human beings, from their mothers' womb, belong to God who searches them and knows them, who forms them and knits them together with his own hands, who gazes on them when they are tiny shapeless embryos and already sees in them the adults of tomorrow whose days are numbered and whose vocation is even now written in the 'book of life' (see *Ps* 139:1, 13-16). There too, when they are still in their mothers' womb — as many passages of the Bible bear witness — they are the personal objects of God's loving and fatherly providence" (n. 61).

The life of every individual is thus part of God's divine plan. Listen to the words of these Old Testament prophets: "Before I formed you in the womb I knew you, / and before you were born I consecrated you" (Jeremiah 1:5) and "Thy hands fashioned and made me; / and now dost thou turn about and destroy me. / Remember that thou hast made me of clay; / and wilt thou turn me to dust again? / Didst thou not pour me out like milk / and curdle me like cheese? / Thou didst clothe me with skin and flesh, / and knit me together with bones and sinews. / Thou hast granted me life and steadfast love; / and thy care has preserved my spirit" (Job 10:8-12).

We know, of course, that it was Jesus Himself who taught very clearly that "unless one is born of water and the Spirit, he cannot enter the kingdom of God" (John 3:5). He was speaking of Baptism and its necessity for salvation. The reason for its necessity is that it washes away the stain of original sin, which we are all born with. The *Catechism of the Catholic Church* states, however, that God has bound salvation to the sacrament of Baptism, but He Himself is not bound by his sacraments. For example, the Church has always held the firm conviction that those who suffer death for the sake of the faith, without having received Baptism, are baptized by their death for and with Christ. Thus, the Baptism of blood, like the desire for Baptism, brings about the fruits of Baptism without being a sacrament. We seen, then, that Baptism is necessary for those to whom the Gospel has been proclaimed and who have had the opportunity to ask for it. And this is why also we believe in the Baptism of desire and the Baptism of blood (see CCC, n. 1257f).

In the case of the unborn, however, neither the child nor the parents are able to ask for Baptism for the child because he or she has not yet even been born. John Paul II emphasizes that it is unthinkable that "even a single moment of this marvelous process of the unfolding of life could be separated from the wise and loving work of the Creator." Knowing all that we do about God and His infinite mercy, the Church is confidently filled with the hope that every innocent, defenseless unborn child is held in the Father's loving arms and that we need not worry about that child's eternal salvation.

Dear Grace,

I already go to church regularly and subscribe to the beliefs of the Catholic religion but wasn't baptized as a child and would like to be now. Is it possible to be baptized as an adult without participating in the year-long inquiry and catechumenate process?

I appreciate your question and I am sure that you have your reasons for asking. Of the seven sacraments of the Catholic Church, Baptism is, of course, extremely important, for it is the entry into the Christian life and no other sacrament may be received without it. As I tell my students, Baptism is like crossing a threshold and, in so doing, we enter into the household of God. As with entering any household, it is a significant step and, once admitted, there will be both privileges and responsibilities. Unfortunately, we often find that many Christians consider Baptism to be merely a ritual, something that one "does" and consequently we do not look beyond at what it means for our entire life.

To answer your question, yes, it is possible to be baptized without participating in the catechumenate process but only with a dispensation from the bishop, which must be requested by the pastor, giving the reasons for the request. In that case, the person would have to demonstrate sufficient knowledge of the Creed, the traditional prayers of the Church, and the Ten Commandments, along with a period of probation (see RCIA, nn. 34.4; 331; Statutes nn. 20, 21). This should demonstrate for us how serious the catechumenate process is. In addition, the Code of Canon Law states the following: "To be baptized, it is required that an adult have manifested the will to receive baptism, be sufficiently instructed in the truths of faith and in Christian obligations and be tested in the Christian life by means of the catechumenate" (canon 865, para. 1).

The *Catechism of the Catholic Church* (n. 1229) tells us that "from the time of the apostles, becoming a Christian has been accomplished by a journey and initiation in several stages. This journey can be covered rapidly or slowly, but certain essential elements will always have to be present: proclamation of the Word, acceptance of the Gospel entailing conversion, profession of faith, Baptism itself, the outpouring of the Holy Spirit, and admission to Eucharistic communion."

You state in your question that you subscribe to the beliefs of the Catholic religion, and this is very good, but if someone stopped you on the street today and asked you why you are Catholic, would you be prepared to give a response? Could you summarize the basic teachings of the Christian faith? For example, what is a sacrament? How do you explain the Incarnation? What is mortal sin? How do we explain the Mother of Jesus to be a perpetual virgin? In cases of extreme necessity, a person could be baptized without knowing the answers to these basic questions; under normal circumstances, however, the person is required to know them. This is not meant to make you feel bad but to challenge you. Even children who are baptized in infancy must undergo a post-baptismal catechumenate before being allowed to receive the other sacraments and be fully initiated in the faith (see CCC, n. 1231).

The Second Vatican Council restored for the Latin Church "the catechumenate for adults, comprising several distinct steps" (*Sacrosanctum Concilium*). The rites for these stages are to be found in the Rite of Christian Initiation of Adults (RCIA). Like a mother, the Church always wants to make sure that we are well prepared for every serious step in our lives. Because Baptism is so essential to our salvation, it will never be denied to anyone requesting it with faith and in serious necessity. If you feel that this describes your situation, then, of course, speak to your pastor right away. If not, then sign up for RCIA. You will discover that there is so much to learn regarding the truth found in the Christian faith. It will change your life.

Dear Grace,

I would like to know when it is acceptable to not receive our Lord at Communion? Is it a sin to miss Communion over venial sin? How long can you go without receiving Communion and still be considered a practicing Catholic? My life has been in great turmoil lately and my thoughts have not been what they should be while I am sorting things out. I really am not sure if I have sinned or not. I really hate to receive our Lord in an unclean vessel right now. Am I wrong to miss Communion?

Thank you for writing. I sense your great concern over this matter. Let me begin by saying that canon law states the following: "All the faithful, after they have been initiated into the Most Holy Eucharist, are bound by the obligation of receiving Communion at least once a year" (canon 920). It is, therefore, not a sin to not receive Communion every Sunday. But it also tells us that "the faithful are to hold the Eucharist in highest honor, taking part in the celebration of the most august Sacrifice, receiving the sacrament devoutly and frequently, and worshiping it with supreme adoration" (canon 898) and that it is those who are "conscious of grave sin" who should not receive the body of the Lord at Mass (see canon 916).

So you see, venial sin should not keep us from receiving the Holy Eucharist. This would be the kind of sin that is not grave. Serious, or grave, sin, on the other hand, is the type that cuts off our communion with God. When we commit that kind of sin, then we must approach the sacrament of Reconciliation and ask forgiveness of God so that our communion and relationship with Him may be restored.

You say that you are having bad thoughts over something that is causing turmoil in your life. It is good that your conscience is leading you to question your actions. Generally speaking, thoughts alone do not constitute grave sin, but we need to be careful with this too. To engage in bad thoughts deliberately without any attempt to avoid them could most definitely — if they go unchecked — lead one to commit a serious sin. But if the thoughts just come as a result of being emotionally upset over a situation that is troubling us, then normally they are not to keep us from receiving Holy Communion.

The best thing to do is to have a talk with your confessor. Sometimes people are uncomfortable doing this, but they should try their best not to be. The priest is there to help us; he wants to offer us the healing power of Jesus. The Eucharist is the very Body and Blood of Christ. It is the "food" we need in this journey called life. That is why Jesus gave Himself to us in this way, so that we would always be united with Him until He returns.

Imagine what would happen to our body if we did not give it food every day. It would eventually die. When we deprive our soul of the food that it needs in the Eucharist, then we are starving it. I understand that you are trying to be very careful and not do something wrong, but when we allow anything to keep us from being united to the Lord in Holy Communion, we are denying ourselves the "food" that we need to truly live.

5

ℒiturgy

Dear Grace,

During Communion at Mass, is it proper to dip the Host into the chalice and then consume it?

Because Jesus Christ Himself is present under the two forms of bread and wine at the Eucharistic Sacrifice, the Church shows them great reverence and sets down specific guidelines as to how Communion is to be received by the faithful. The "ordinary" ministers of the Eucharist are bishops, priests, and deacons. Ordinarily, they too "receive" Communion from another minister, with the exception of the principal celebrant. This is because, in our tradition, Communion is always "received" and never "taken." Thus, those delegated to be "extraordinary" ministers of Communion must themselves first receive Communion before distributing it to others.

The practice of dipping the Host into the chalice is called "intinction." It is not a recommended method. But if this method is used, obviously the recipient must receive it on the tongue due to the danger of drops falling. When Communion is distributed under both kinds by intinction, the Host is not placed in the hands of the communicant, nor may the communicant "take" the Host and dip it into the chalice. If the person is handed the Host, and for some reason is not able to drink from the cup, then he or she must give it to a priest, deacon, or other minister to be dipped into the Precious Blood on his or her behalf. This way, the individual would not be self-administering (see *General Instruction of the Roman Missal*, n. 287).

One thing to keep in mind is that it is not required to receive Communion under both forms. Even though this is accepted and practiced today, as in the early Church, our doctrine from the Council of Trent regarding this has not changed. The Catholic Church teaches that Jesus Christ is completely and entirely present under both forms and therefore the effects are complete, whether one receives under either form of bread or wine alone or together.

So, if there is some reason why we cannot drink from the cup, then we certainly have the option of taking Communion under the form of bread alone (see *General Instruction of the Roman Missal*, n. 284, c.). This way, we will be showing great reverence for our Lord by avoiding a practice that would resemble "self-communicating."

Dear Grace,

During the Mass, is it permissible for extraordinary ministers of the Eucharist to give Communion to themselves under the species of wine? In other words, are they permitted to approach the altar on their "own" initiative and take the chalice into their own hands without first "receiving" it from another minister?

What this question refers to is the whole notion of self-communication — when a person gives Communion to himself. This is never permissible (see *General Instruction of the Roman Missal*, n. 160). Only the celebrant of the Mass takes the Host and the chalice by himself. He "gives" it to the concelebrants and deacons as well as to the faithful assembled. What is important to keep in mind here is that, as we have said previously, there is no "taking" of Communion, rather only a "reception" of Communion. The grace that Christ offers us in these mysteries is initiated by Him, not by us. Therefore, we may never attempt to give the Eucharist to ourselves.

Extraordinary ministers of the Eucharist perform a great service in assisting at Mass when needed, but we must never confuse their role with that of the priest or deacon. They are properly called "extraordinary" ministers because they are not the norm. When there is no ordained minister present and there are a truly great number of communicants, the priest may call upon extraordinary ministers to assist him. In cases of necessity, he may also commission suitable members of the faithful for this occasion (see *General Instruction of the Roman Missal*, n. 162). The "ordinary" minister of Holy Communion at Mass and outside of Mass is the ordained bishop, priest, or deacon. After them, an instituted acolyte is the most appropriate. Only the principal celebrant of the Mass, whether a bishop or a priest, may "self-communicate."

So, the answer is no. Extraordinary ministers of the Eucharist may never give Communion from the chalice to themselves. They must always "receive" Christ from an authorized minister of the cup, not necessarily the principal celebrant.

More importantly, let us focus on the fact that in the Church all the Christian faithful possess a true equality with regard to dignity, and we all have different roles that have been willed by Christ in order for the members of His Body to serve the Church's unity and mission (see CCC, n. 872). We are all one Body, and each one of us is very important in God's eyes.

Dear Grace,

Is hand-holding during the Our Father at Mass encouraged or is it to be discouraged? I can find no mention of hand-holding in the Roman Missal or the Sacramentary.

The holding of hands during the Our Father, or Lord's Prayer, during the Mass is a gesture that has developed and grown over the years. It is not found in the rubrics or Church legislation governing the celebration of Mass. Although it is true that a priest or deacon must not change the wording and the gestures, if the people wish to be more expressive it appears they may do so. Many Catholics, however, are quite uncomfortable with the whole notion of holding hands with someone they do not know.

Another gesture that many Catholics are in the habit of doing is that of extending their hands upward in an *orans* position along with the priest at the time of the Our Father. (*Orans* is Latin for "one who prays.") And it is this gesture that the bishops of the United States have proposed to be included in the new Sacramentary. We do not have, however, an official liturgical norm on this practice as of this date. The United States Bishops' Committee on the Liturgy expressed a strong preference for the *orans* gesture over the holding of hands, since the focus of the Lord's Prayer is a prayer prayed to the Father and is not primarily an expression of community and fellowship.

Some may feel also that hand-holding detracts from the "exchange of peace" that comes a little later in the Communion rite. Perhaps if we better understood the theology underlying the *orans* position, more people would prefer it to holding hands.

Dear Grace,

Is it proper to kneel at Mass after the *Agnus Dei* (or Lamb of God) until Communion? The Roman Missal does not indicate we should.

The Holy Sacrifice of the Mass is divided into two major parts — the Liturgy of the Word and the Liturgy of the Eucharist. The question of when we are to kneel pertains to the second part, the Liturgy of the Eucharist. During this portion of the Mass, there are two points where Catholics of the Roman Rite want to know about kneeling — the Consecration and the Communion rite of the whole Eucharistic Prayer. There has been much confusion about the rules and a wide variation in practice. Your question refers to kneeling during the Communion rite.

Until recently, the *General Instruction of the Roman Missal* had made no reference to kneeling after the *Agnus Dei*, or Lamb of God, until Communion. This, however, has now changed. On November 14, 2001, the United States Conference of Catholic Bishops proposed some adaptations to the 2000 edition of the *General Instruction of the Roman Missal* for the dioceses of the United States. Some of these adaptations were approved in a decree by the Congregation for Divine Worship and the Discipline of the

Sacraments on April 17, 2002, and will be inserted into future editions of the Roman Missal in English for use in those dioceses.

Regarding kneeling, the adaptations state: "In the dioceses of the United States of America, [the faithful] should kneel beginning after the singing or recitation of the Sanctus until after the Amen of the Eucharistic Prayer, except when prevented on occasion by reasons of health, lack of space, the large number of people present, or some other good reason. Those who do not kneel ought to make a profound bow when the priest genuflects after the consecration. The faithful kneel after the *Agnus Dei* unless the Diocesan Bishop determines otherwise" (*General Instruction of the Roman Missal*, n. 43). So, we see that kneeling after the *Agnus Dei* is now a liturgical norm in the dioceses of the United States.

For many centuries, Catholics have expressed their reverence for the Body and Blood of Christ present on the altar by the practice of kneeling during both the Consecration and the Communion rite. It was not until some time after the Second Vatican Council that an attempt was made by some liturgists to change the people's customary posture during Mass. It does seem, however, that kneeling during the Communion rite has been a custom and an act of personal piety that Catholics in America have almost universally continued to practice by kneeling from the end of the *Agnus Dei* until they go to receive Communion, and even after receiving until the final prayer and blessing, in spite of the legal technicality that it was not required. Now, it has finally been written into the liturgical law of the Church for the dioceses in the United States. One can say that the faithful have always done this out of sincere love for the Lord and as an expression of their belief in the Real Presence of Christ in the Eucharist.

Dear Grace,

Is a crucifix with the figure of the crucified Lord required at all Masses? Can it be replaced by a cross with the risen Lord on it?

According to the *General Instruction of the Roman Missal* (n. 308), "There is to be a cross, with the figure of Christ crucified upon it, positioned either on the altar or near it, and which is clearly visible to the people gathered together. It is fitting that a cross of this kind, recalling for the faithful the saving passion of the Lord, remain near the altar even outside of liturgical celebrations." So, the answer is no. A cross with a risen Christ may not replace a crucifix during Mass.

The *Ceremonial of Bishops* (n. 128) comments that the image on the cross is to face forward. In the Latin version, which is the authoritative version, "cross" is *crux*. This has traditionally, in our Church, meant a "crucifix." The same word is used in documents before and after the Second Vatican Council. Had a new interpretation of this word been intended, surely some mention would have been made in the official documents. A cross with the risen Christ does not fulfill the requirement for a crucifix. It is not prohibited, however, to have an image of a risen Christ or a plain cross without a corpus elsewhere in the church or even behind the altar as long as during Mass itself a crucifix is "on or near the altar" at all times.

The Mass may be described in many different ways, but above all, it is a sacrifice. The Lord instituted this memorial of His sacrifice so that we would remember and never forget what He accomplished for us on the cross and why He did it. It took love to die for us as He did. In the Mass, we encounter that love, and hopefully we will be so moved that we, too, will go out into the world and strive to love as He did.

Dear Grace,

Why do some people genuflect in front of the Eucharistic minister before receiving Communion?

You understand, of course, that they are not genuflecting to the Eucharistic minister but to Christ truly present in the sacred Host. The Church has always required that the faithful show respect and reverence for the Eucharist at the moment of receiving it. When you see people genuflecting before receiving Communion, it is because they are trying to show the reverence that is required, but perhaps they are not doing it at the proper moment.

The latest adaptations to the *General Instruction of the Roman Missal* for the dioceses of the United States were approved by the Congregation for Divine Worship and the Discipline of the Sacraments on April 17, 2002, and are now in force. They state the following: "The norm for reception of Holy Communion in the dioceses of the United States is standing. Communicants [however] should not be denied Holy Communion because they kneel. Rather, such instances should be addressed pastorally, by providing the faithful with proper catechesis on the reasons for this norm. When receiving Holy Communion in the hand, the communicant bows his or her head before the sacrament as a gesture of reverence and receives the Body of the Lord from the minister. The consecrated host may be received either on the tongue or in the hand at the discretion of each communicant. When Holy Communion is received under both kinds, the sign of reverence is also made before receiving the Precious Blood" (*General Instruction of the Roman Missal*, n. 160).

In other words, if a person is going to receive Communion standing — as is now the norm — but he or she wishes to genuflect, then perhaps the person should make this sign of reverence when he or she is one or two persons back in the line before reaching the Eucharistic minister. If one chooses to receive kneeling, then no other sign of reverence is necessary, since the kneeling itself is the sign of supreme adoration. It is wonderful that we have so many coming up to receive our Lord. Because we have so many, however, we need to be mindful of how to do things so that the beautiful flow in our liturgy is maintained, while at the same time showing God the reverence that we so desire to give.

Dear Grace,

As a Catholic who attends Mass regularly, I have always been curious about something. What is the meaning behind the

making of the sign of the cross on the forehead, lips, and heart before the reading of the Gospel at Mass?

You would be surprised at how many people wonder about this gesture. When we hear the Gospel proclaimed, we are hearing God Himself speak to us. We sign ourselves on the forehead to express a desire that the Lord would be in our mind; on the lips, that He might be in our speech; and on our hearts, that He might be in our heart. The Scriptures are the living Word of God, and the Gospels contain Jesus' words. We would never want for them to fall on closed minds, lips, or hearts. The sign of the cross is always a sign of our love, honor, and respect for God and also a reminder of the great love that He showed us in laying down His life so that we might live.

Dear Grace,

What is the meaning of the rose candle lit on the Third Sunday of Advent?

The Third Sunday of Advent is called *Gaudete* ("Rejoice") Sunday from the first word of the Opening Prayer at Mass. The season of Advent originated as a fast of forty days in preparation for Christmas. By the twelfth century, the fast had been replaced by simple abstinence; but Advent still preserved most of the characteristics of a penitential season, which made it a kind of counterpart to Lent, with the middle or third Sunday corresponding with *Laetare* or Mid-Lent Sunday. On that day, as on *Laetare* Sunday, the organ and flowers, forbidden during the rest of the season, were permitted to be used. Rose-colored vestments for the clergy are allowed instead of violet. *Gaudete* Sunday, like *Laetare* Sunday, comes about midway through a season that is otherwise of a penitential character. It signifies the nearness of the Lord's coming.

Dear Grace,

Can blue replace violet as the liturgical color during Advent?

Blue is not a normative liturgical color and has only been given special use in Mexico for Marian feasts. Elsewhere it is also frequently used in conjunction with white on Marian feast days. Advent is a season of penance, meant to prepare the faithful for the coming of Christ. There is no Church document permitting blue to replace violet during Advent. According to the *General Instruction of the Roman Missal*, "Traditional usage should be retained for the vestment colors. . . . [d.] Violet is used in Advent and Lent. It may also be worn in offices and Masses for the dead" (n. 346). Wearing bluish-purple would perhaps be permitted, but "pure blue" would not. Violet is the traditional penitential color. Rose may be used, where it is the custom, on *Gaudete* Sunday, or Third Sunday of Advent (see *General Instruction of the Roman Missal*, n. 346, f.).

Advent is a time of preparation, waiting, and hope. The Advent liturgy resounds with the longing cries of the Hebrew prophets, the voice of Jesus, and John the Baptist's preaching that the Lord is near. We still hear their message ringing through today's dark winters. The stories told in the Gospels for the Sundays of Advent should help us listen to their voices.

Dear Grace,

Is it permissible during Mass for a priest to replace the Nicene Creed with his "own" version of what we believe?

If you are talking about a priest making up his own creed, or profession of faith, then the answer is no. This would never be permissible because it would not be the authentic and authoritative expression of the faith of the Catholic Church. The Church tells us that the creed "was not made to accord with human opinions, but rather what was of the greatest importance was gathered from all the Scriptures, to present the one teaching of the faith in its entirety" (CCC, n. 186). Even though the purpose for changing the words of the creed might be to help people to better understand it, there is still the risk of causing confusion or the possibility of falling into error.

"The symbol or profession of faith serves as a way for all the people gathered together to respond to the word of God proclaimed in the readings taken from Sacred Scripture and explained in the homily, and so that, by professing the rule of faith in a formula approved for liturgical use, the great mysteries of the faith may be recalled and confirmed before their celebration in the Eucharist is begun" (*General Instruction of the Roman Missal*, n. 67). Other forms of the Nicene Creed may be used but only those that have been approved by the Church.

Dear Grace,

My son approached me with a question, but I do not know if I answered him to the fullest. He wanted to know why it is that we have Lent and also why we do not fast for the entire forty days. Could you please explain the message behind Lent and why we do not fast every single day of the forty days?

As Christians, in everything we do, we should have as our model Jesus Christ. Scripture tells us that "Jesus was led up by the Spirit into the wilderness to be tempted by the devil. And he fasted forty days and forty nights" (Matthew 4:1-2). The season of Lent is a commemoration of our Lord's fast, which He undertook before entering into His public ministry. It was a time of preparation for the tremendous mission that lay before Him. To do this, He denied Himself food and water during those forty days and nights, relying instead only on God, with whom He was one, to sustain Him.

In the history of the Church, Lent has undergone some development and change, both in duration and in practice. In other words, it was not always forty days in length, and the fast was not always observed in the same way. For example, during the late second century, the season of penance before Easter was much shorter and some people fasted for one day, others for two days, and others for a greater number of days. The first clear mention and observance of the forty days does not come to us until the fourth century in the decrees of the Council of Nicaea, in 325.

What we see from some of the earliest references is that originally the season of Lent was meant as a preparation for Baptism or as a time in which people sought absolution from God for their sins. Even though fasting and abstinence were part of the practice, there was no uniform manner in which this was done. That came later. It was observed differently in various countries, and in Rome, where it had been customarily three weeks, it was eventually extended to six weeks, but always leaving out the Sundays. Because this made the Lenten season only thirty-six days in duration, with time it was lengthened by adding four more days, making it forty, in remembrance of Jesus' fast in the desert, and it has been observed this way by much of the Catholic Church since the seventh century.

You ask in your letter why we do not fast the entire forty days of Lent. In reality, we are to fast all forty days. On November 18, 1966, the National Conference of Catholic Bishops, in keeping with the letter and spirit of Pope Paul's constitution *Paenitemini*, published some norms on penitential observance. In one part of the document, they specifically wrote about what is expected and recommended for all Catholics during the entire season of Lent. They stated: "We ask, urgently and prayerfully, that we, as people of God, make of the entire Lenten season a period of special penitential observance."

In addition to making it clear that we are bound by obligation to fast and abstain from meat on Ash Wednesday and Good Friday and to abstain from meat on every Friday of Lent, they also added the following: "For all other weekdays of Lent, we strongly recommend participation in daily Mass and a self-imposed observance of fasting." Remembering that fasting is a form of penance and self-denial, we must keep in mind that we are urged to do this during the entire season of Lent, but it does not have to be a fast from food on all those forty days. There are many other ways in which we can show God how sorry we are for our sins. Among them are being generous with others, visiting the sick and lonely, feeding the poor, studying Scripture, participating in the Stations of the Cross, praying the Rosary, practicing self-control, and many others.

Even when the United States bishops made it no longer required to abstain from meat on Fridays, they never intended that the Catholic faithful should discontinue this practice. What they hoped for was that people would continue to do it out of their love for God and not because they had to, and also to give us an opportunity to deny ourselves in other ways. Friday has never ceased to be a day of penance and self-denial, and abstaining from meat on that day is given first place because it was on a Friday that our Lord died for our sins. Every Friday is a day to prepare for Sunday, the day that, for us who believe, is Easter every week of the year. And Sunday should never be a day of fasting, not even during Lent. It is always the glorious Day of the Lord!

Dear Grace,

A Jewish friend of mine pointed out a supposed problem with the Christian concept of the Last Supper. As we all know, Jesus gave His disciples bread and wine during that Passover meal. My friend claims that bread is never served during the Passover meal. Is that correct? If so, what effect does it have on the Church's position on the Eucharist?

Since ancient times, the Jewish people have celebrated the salvific, or saving, acts of God in their lives in the feast of the Passover, and this very sacred holiday included the *Seder* meal. It was this meal that Jesus, being a Jew, shared with His Apostles on the night before He died. This was the Last Supper. The ritual for this meal was prescribed by God to Moses and Aaron, and it is recounted in the twelfth chapter of the Book of Exodus. Bread was most definitely a part of the meal, but it had to be unleavened bread made without yeast or any other leavening agent that causes the dough to rise (see Exodus 12:8).

Perhaps your friend is assuming, for some reason, that Jesus did not use unleavened bread at the Last Supper when He instituted the Eucharist. The New Testament tells us, however: "Now on the first day of Unleavened Bread the disciples came to Jesus, saying,

'Where will you have us prepare for you to eat the passover?' "
(Matthew 26:17; see also Mark 14:12 and Luke 22:1). Then, we
also read that "when the hour came, he sat at table, and the apostles
with him. And he said to them, 'I have earnestly desired to eat this
passover with you before I suffer' " (Luke 22:14-15).

Scripture goes on to say that Jesus "took bread, and when he
had given thanks he broke it and gave it to them, saying, 'This is
my body which is given for you. Do this in remembrance of me' "
(Luke 22:19). During the Passover feast, the eating of or even
contact with anything with leaven was strictly forbidden. God had
instructed them, "Seven days you shall eat unleavened bread; on
the first day you shall put away leaven out of your houses, for if any
one eats what is leavened from the first day until the seventh day,
that person shall be cut off from Israel" (Exodus 12:15). It is quite
clear, therefore, that Jesus did indeed celebrate the Jewish Passover
meal with His Apostles and that unleavened bread was eaten. To
this day, the bread used for the Eucharistic sacrifice in the liturgy
of the Roman Rite must be unleavened (see *General Instruction of
the Roman Missal*, nn. 320, 321).

It seems that some people do not realize how closely linked the
Catholic Mass is to the Jewish Passover, or *Seder* meal. This is
precisely where the Mass has its roots. The God of Israel had given
very specific directions regarding how the meal was to be prepared.
One very important element was the lamb. Each family was to
slaughter a year-old male lamb without blemish (see Exodus 12:5),
the most perfect lamb they could find. Some of the blood of the
lamb was to be applied to the doorposts of every house in order to
protect the Israelites when the Lord would come to destroy the
Egyptians. The rest of the lamb was to be roasted and eaten on that
day. After this, they were to keep this as a memorial feast for all
generations to come, as a perpetual institution (see Exodus 12:14).

On the night when Jesus celebrated this traditional Jewish
meal with His Apostles, something very different happened. This
time He gave them the bread that He had blessed and said, "This
is my body" (Matthew 26:26; Luke 22:19). Thus, He became the

sacrificial, unblemished lamb without sin. This is why Jesus is called the Lamb of God. Both the Jewish Passover and the Last Supper, which we now call the Mass or Eucharist, are memorials of the salvation of God's people. Let us pray that one day God may find us sharing this meal together at His Table, united by that love which He has placed in our hearts.

Dear Grace,

I hear Catholics talking so much about Holy Week. What exactly is going on during this time?

Holy Week is definitely a very sacred time of the year, for it is then that we commemorate and remember the last week of Jesus' life on this earth. These are the days leading up to the great Easter Feast. The Lenten season of sacrifice and self-denial is about to come to an end, and this week is extremely important for all Christians. The greatest focus of the week is the suffering, Passion, and Resurrection of Jesus Christ and all the events that lead up to it.

Historical documents tell us that as early as the fourth century the Church celebrated this "Great Week" with a feeling of profound sanctity. It begins with Passion Sunday, sometimes referred to popularly as "Palm Sunday," which marks Jesus' triumphant entry into Jerusalem. The central feature of the service proper to this day, as it was in the earliest times, is the procession with palms. The palms are blessed and are then usually borne in procession to the church, where an entry is made with a certain amount of ceremony, after which the Mass is celebrated. The other notable and ancient feature of the present Palm Sunday service is the reading of the Gospel of the Passion by three narrators.

Especially important for Catholics is the Easter Triduum. These are the three days just before Easter. On Holy Thursday we reenact the Lord's Last Supper, which He shared with His Apostles on the night He was betrayed and arrested. Surely this is one of the most beautiful liturgies of the entire liturgical year. At the Mass, the priest washes the feet of twelve men, just as Jesus did. Also on this night, priests all over the world will renew their priestly commitment. This is because, at the Last Supper, Jesus not only instituted the Eucharist, the Mass, but also the ministerial priesthood.

On Good Friday, the day of the crucifixion and death of our Lord, we have the Veneration of the Cross. A service is held at the hour when he died, at three o'clock in the afternoon, and another later in the evening. We go forward and kiss the cross in order to show honor and respect for Christ's sacrifice for our sake. There is no consecration of the Eucharist on this day. The Communion we receive will be from the night before, which has been reserved in the tabernacle.

Holy Saturday ends with a vigil. We keep watch for the expectant rising of our Savior. This was the day He went down into the netherworld in order to raise up with Him those who had died before His coming. Up to this time, the gates to heaven were closed and no one could be admitted there because of the original sin of Adam. Jesus changed all that. By paying the price for our sins on the cross, He gained for us our eternal salvation, and heaven was opened once more. Also, on this night, candidates who have spent months of preparation will be received through Baptism and Confirmation into the Catholic Church. It is a joyous occasion.

Those who engage themselves wholeheartedly in living the entire paschal cycle of Lent, the Easter Triduum, and the subsequent fifty days, discover that it can change them forever! This is especially so of the Triduum. It stands at the heart of the Easter season and is an intense immersion in the fundamental mystery of what it means to be Christian. During these days we suffer with Christ so that we might rise with Him at His glorious Resurrection. Holy Week is a time to clear our schedules of unnecessary activities. Our minds and hearts should be fixed on Jesus and what He did for us. Let us bear the cross so that we may be worthy of wearing the crown He wears.

Dear Grace,

Could you please tell me if there is a specific point in the Mass at which we are required to kneel? I see people doing different things and I am confused about it.

Thank you for your letter. It shows that you have a sincere concern about the proper way to adore the Lord in the Sacred Liturgy. Until recently, the Catholic faithful were only required to kneel at the Consecration, but with the adaptations to the *General Instruction of the Roman Missal*, we now have new liturgical norms that require kneeling after the *Agnus Dei* (or Lamb of God).

As pointed out elsewhere in this book, here is what one of those adaptations says: "In the dioceses of the United States of America, [the faithful] should kneel beginning after the singing or recitation of the Sanctus until after the Amen of the Eucharistic Prayer, except when prevented on occasion by reasons of health, lack of space, the large number of people present, or some other good reason. Those who do not kneel ought to make a profound bow when the priest genuflects after the consecration. The faithful kneel after the *Agnus Dei* unless the Diocesan Bishop determines otherwise" (*General Instruction of the Roman Missal*, n. 43).

The *General Instruction of the Roman Missal* (n. 3) states that the Mass "proclaims the sublime mystery of the Lord's real presence under the Eucharistic elements" and that "the Mass does this not only by means of the very words of consecration, by which Christ becomes truly present through transubstantiation, but also by the spirit and expression of reverence and adoration in which the Eucharistic liturgy is carried out." What this means is that we, as a worshipping people, at least in part express our belief that Jesus is present by our action and posture during this point in the liturgy.

Canon law tells us that the faithful are to hold the Eucharist in highest honor, taking part in the celebration of the "most august Sacrifice" and we are to worship it with "supreme adoration" (canon 898). From earliest times, kneeling has always been an act of adoration. In the Garden of Gethsemane, even Jesus knelt down to pray to the Father (see Luke 22:41). There are many other references of people kneeling before God in the Scriptures (see Acts 9:40, 20:36, 21:5).

There are some circumstances that would make kneeling very difficult. For example, when Mass is celebrated in a very crowded place or outdoors or in a stadium. In these situations, however, you will still see some people who will wish to kneel, even on the bare floor. In doing so, they are trying to display their supreme adoration of our Lord and to take full part in this most sacred moment of the liturgy. We should keep in mind, of course, that all forms of adoration are seen and accepted by God, and He blesses every action of ours when our hearts are filled with love.

Dear Grace,

I am a convert and have wanted to ask this for a long time. Why does the Catholic Church not teach the children separately on Sundays? There are so many lessons from the Old Testament that can be taught. For example, Moses, Noah, Job, Ruth, the Ten Commandments, to name only a few. There are even more "lessons" that Jesus taught that should be expressly taught to the children — for example, the Good Samaritan, the Loaves and the Fishes, the Good Shepherd, Faith and the Mustard Seed, and others.

Thank you for writing. I am happy to tell you that many parishes do exactly as you are suggesting. As we know, the Mass is divided into two main parts: the Liturgy of the Word and the Liturgy of the Eucharist. It is during the Liturgy of the Word when the Word of God is read and the homily or sermon is given that children can be taken to a separate place in the church so that they may hear the Word of God and have it explained to them at their level. After that, they return and rejoin the entire congregation for the celebration of the remainder of the Mass.

It always takes interested and willing people to make a children's liturgy possible. If you feel strongly about it, please consider speaking to the Director of Religious Education at your parish. I am certain that he or she will gladly welcome your suggestions and assistance. May the Lord bless you and your family.

Dear Grace,

When I enter a church, should I genuflect toward the altar, the crucifix, or the tabernacle?

In a church, and during liturgical services, there are two primary gestures that are practiced by the congregation. These are genuflecting and bowing. The act of genuflection, which is made by the bending of the right knee to the ground, is an expression of supreme adoration and reverence, and therefore it is reserved to God alone. When we enter a church and there is a tabernacle (the receptacle in which the Blessed Sacrament is reserved) in the sanctuary, whether on the altar or close by, then without hesitation we should genuflect toward it in acknowledgment of the Real Presence of the Lord therein.

The *General Instruction of the Roman Missal*, which legislates for Eucharistic celebrations, states that if there is a tabernacle with the Blessed Sacrament in the sanctuary, a genuflection is made whenever anyone passes in front of the Blessed Sacrament, unless the person is involved in a procession (see n. 274). In other words, the major times we need to be concerned about genuflecting is before and after Mass or when entering and leaving a church or chapel when there is a tabernacle with the Blessed Sacrament present.

During Mass the congregation should have no real reason to pass the Blessed Sacrament, since we are not walking around. At Communion, however, some sign of respect and reverence is required toward the presence of Jesus in the Holy Eucharist, though it must be done at the proper moment. If one is receiving Communion standing, then a bow is made before being offered the sacred Host. If one is kneeling, then no other sign of reverence is necessary. A person may choose to genuflect, bow, or make a sign of the cross when he or she is, let us say, one or two persons away from the ordained minister or the extraordinary minister of the Eucharist. This is done so that the order of people going to and from Communion is not disrupted (see *General Instruction of the Roman Missal*, nn. 160, 274).

There is one situation in which the faithful would genuflect to the Lord's holy cross. This would be from the solemn adoration in the liturgy of Good Friday until the beginning of the Easter Vigil (see *General Instruction of the Roman Missal*, n. 274).

Traditionally, a genuflection is also made before a relic of the holy cross when it is exposed for veneration.

In the Roman Rite of the Church, there are two kinds of bows — the bow of the body (the deep, or profound, bow) and the bow of the head. When there is no tabernacle in the main sanctuary, the appropriate gesture is a deep bow (when the body bends from the waist) to the altar (see *General Instruction of the Roman Missal*, n. 275). This is done out of reverence for the place upon which the Eucharistic sacrifice will take place.

Perhaps the reason for the confusion regarding whether to genuflect or bow to the altar comes from the fact that many of the faithful are still practicing what they were accustomed to do when the tabernacle used to be located on or behind the altar. It is usually our human nature to be inclined to do what seems most familiar to us, even after the Church has asked for a change.

Genuflection and bowing are beautiful gestures by which we express our adoration and reverence to God. He sent His only Son into the world to save us from our own sinfulness. Christ then promised never to leave us, and in the Holy Eucharist we have the fulfillment of that promise. There, He is present — Body, Blood, Soul, and Divinity. What an honor and privilege to bend the knee or bow before Him!

Dear Grace,

I would like to know what is behind the practice of abstaining from meat on the Fridays of Lent. Being a Catholic, I was asked that question and I was unable to answer it. Please answer this in your column during Lent if possible.

Abstinence from or depriving oneself of certain foods has been a part of the history of man since the beginning. God said to the first man, Adam, that he should not eat from the tree of the knowledge of good and evil, lest he die (see Genesis 2:16). It is generally understood that this was so that man would always recognize his dependence on his Creator. But Adam disobeyed

God and this sin, as St. Augustine explained, was transmitted to all his descendants. Penance thus became necessary in order to make up to God for the transgression against Him. The Jews, therefore, enacted laws that would satisfy this necessity for penance.

To the Jewish people, laws regarding fasting pertained to the amount of food to be eaten, while laws regarding abstinence pertained to the quality or kind of food. Their many difficult times and hardships led them to take on the burden of fasting and abstinence because they believed that it was pleasing to God and would bring them closer to Him. Abstinence from meat appears to be grounded in the directive to Noah and his sons by God that "only you shall not eat flesh with its life, that is, its blood" (Genesis 9:4). The people of ancient times regarded blood as the seat of life and therefore sacred. Thus, abstaining from eating the meat of red-blooded animals became a law to be observed on certain days of penance.

We know, of course, that Jesus prepared for His public ministry by fasting for forty days and nights in the desert. Although, during His time with them, He did not give specific directions as to how His followers were to fast after His Ascension to the Father, it is quite evident that fasting and abstinence were faithfully adhered to by the first Christians (see Acts 13:3, 14:23) and that they also practiced the abstinence from meat, continuing the prohibition of the Mosaic Law (see Acts 15:20, 29).

Since the early days of Christianity, Friday has been recognized as a day of fasting and abstinence in memory of the fact that the Lord Jesus Christ suffered and died on that day of the week. The manner in which it has been observed, however, has undergone some change. In current Church practice in the United States, all those fourteen years of age and above are bound to refrain from eating meat on those days prescribed as "penitential" — Ash Wednesday, Good Friday, and the Fridays of Lent.

In a statement called "Penitential Practices for Today's Catholics," the Committee on Pastoral Practices of the National Conference of Catholic Bishops stated the following: "Recalling our Lord's Passion and death on Good Friday, we hold all Fridays to have special significance. Jesus' self-denial and self-offering invite us to enter freely into His experience by forgoing food, bearing humiliations, and forgiving those who injure us. Through the grace of the Holy Spirit, the principal agent of all spiritual transformation, this can be done — and done with a spirit of quiet joy. For Christians, suffering and joy are not incompatible."

So, you see, you can tell your friend that when we deny ourselves meat on the Fridays of Lent we are doing something that is rooted in Scripture and the history of the Christian Church. We join Christ on His journey to Jerusalem and say no to ourselves as He did. Not eating meat on Friday is but a small thing when compared to the sacrifice He made by laying down His life willingly so that we might live.

Dear Grace,

I have always wanted to know if we fulfill the Sunday Mass obligation when we arrive late. Is there a point during the Mass at which it is too late to attend?

This is a good question because often today there is a tendency to think that as long as we have arrived in time to receive Communion, then we have fulfilled our Sunday obligation to keep holy the Lord's Day. But there is a great deal more to it than that. When a person is careless about being on time for Mass, especially when this happens repeatedly, it can be a sign that there is a lack of understanding of the action that is taking place at the Mass. This needs to be thought out carefully.

The Holy Sacrifice of the Mass is made up of two parts, the Liturgy of the Word and the Liturgy of the Eucharist, and these two parts make up the whole Mass. It is during the Liturgy of the Eucharist (the second part) that we receive our Lord in Holy Communion, but there is something else that will take place before that happens. In the first part (the Liturgy of the Word) God will reach out to us. This is accomplished through the readings from Sacred Scripture. Every part of the Mass is important, but this is especially important because when the lector approaches the ambo to read, we should know that we are about to hear God speak through the Scriptures.

It is stated in the documents of the Second Vatican Council that "the Church has always venerated the Scriptures just as she venerates the body of the Lord, since, especially in sacred liturgy, she unceasingly receives and offers to the faithful the bread of life from the table both of God's Word and of Christ's body. She has always maintained them, and continues to do so, together with sacred tradition, as the supreme rule of faith. . . . Therefore, like the Christian religion itself, all the preaching of the Church must be nourished and regulated by Sacred Scripture. For, in the sacred books, the Father who is in heaven meets His children with great love and speaks with them" (*Dei Verbum*, n. 21).

In a document published in 1980, the Congregation for Divine Worship and the Discipline of the Sacraments stated the following: " 'The two parts which in a sense go to make up the Mass, namely the liturgy of the word and the Eucharistic liturgy, are so closely connected that they form but one single act of worship.' A person should not approach the table of the bread of the Lord without having first been at the table of his word. Sacred Scripture is therefore of the highest importance in the celebration of Mass" (*Inaestimabile Donum*, n. 1).

The Mass is both a sacrificial memorial of the sacrifice of Christ on the cross and a "sacred banquet of communion with the Lord's body and blood" (CCC, n. 1382). Foremost, it is a sacrifice, but it is also a meal. The sacrifice is memorialized so that by remembering what He did for us, we might be transformed to go out into the world and love as He did, and Christ's own flesh and blood give us the nourishment and strength needed to do this. Perhaps if we think of this aspect, it might become clearer to us why it is wrong to arrive only in time to go up to the table and eat, thinking that to be the only nourishment we need. In reality, however, the table to which the Lord invites us feeds us with both His Word and His Body and Blood.

Every effort should be made to be on time for Mass. If we are not able to be present in time to be seated for the readings from the Word of God, then it might be better to plan to attend the next available Mass on that day. If we rush in just in time for Communion, then we will not have truly experienced the transforming sacrifice of Jesus. We will not have been completely nourished by the Lord's Word and His Body and Blood. If we who love Him so had been there on the day He died, would we have been late?

Dear Grace,

It pains me to see that reverent silence is almost no longer observed in church before or after Mass for the benefit of people who wish to prepare spiritually before Mass or make a fitting thanksgiving for Communion after Mass. I was taught to observe reverence in silence before Jesus, who is truly present in the Tabernacle. Even in a church that has a "no talking in church" sign in the vestibule, people start visiting, even in loud voices, as soon as Father leaves in procession. Please address this issue, which is a source of much grief for me.

It is clear that you are expressing a deeply felt concern — one that I am certain flows from a profound love for God. Reverence for God, even in His own house, is something so often forgotten in today's fast-paced world. How often do we consider, for example, that every time we enter the church, we actually step, in a sense, into heaven? There, we receive a foretaste, or hint, of the place for which we are destined — the holy city, the heavenly Jerusalem.

We are also reminded that a church is a house of prayer where the sacrifice of Jesus our Savior is offered and where He remains present in the tabernacle even after the celebration of the Eucharist (see CCC, n. 1181). Therefore, every time we enter a church, we should show utter respect and reverence, especially before and after the Eucharistic Sacrifice of the Mass.

The Mass is the highest form of prayer possible. The entire Mass is a prayer. We should want, therefore, to "pray" the Mass, not simply attend the Mass. In order to do this, we must prepare ourselves properly. This actually can begin from as early as the evening before by spending some amount of time, even briefly, in quiet meditation. To think that, the following day, you will be united bodily with your Savior, with your God!

When we arrive at church, we should also be mindful of the quiet time that others may wish to have as they prepare for Mass, and after Mass as well. If we must talk for a very important reason, it should be done in a low voice, so as to not disturb others around us. It shows lack of respect and reverence when we "chit-chat," laugh, and joke in church. And a large number of us are guilty of it! There are many moments that make up the liturgy. Some are vocal, but some clearly call for silence.

The presence of Christ in the Eucharist begins from the moment of the consecration and lasts for as long as the Eucharistic species subsist (see CCC, n. 1377). We need to consider, therefore, that (as with food) it may take fifteen to twenty minutes before our body is completely absorbed into the host we have consumed. We say it this way because Jesus is not absorbed into us; we are absorbed into Him; we become more like Him. So, for those fifteen to twenty minutes after Communion, we should be in awe, almost in rapture, not rushing to leave or to talk. This reverence for God requires stillness of the heart and mind, and this is made possible through quiet, peaceful silence. To achieve it, it must be practiced. Once it is mastered, however, we will wonder how we ever lived without it.

6
Morality

Dear Grace,

I know that many Christian churches require their members to give ten percent of their earnings in the form of a "tithe," but where does the Catholic Church stand on this?

Your question reminds me of a little story I heard recently. It goes like this: A one-dollar bill and a twenty-dollar bill were talking. The twenty-dollar bill was telling the one-dollar bill what fantastic times he always has; he goes to the best restaurants, to the theater, the opera, etc. The one-dollar bill said, "How wonderful and interesting your life is. All I ever get to do is go to church." Many of us would have to agree how true that story is!

In speaking about tithing and what we should give to the Church, we often forget that everything we have already belongs to God. Our money and possessions are not ours but His. All that we have is ours only because He allows us to have it! If we in the world today were to place God first in our lives, there would be no question or problem about tithes because our hearts would be filled with charity and we would give to and support the Church in the best way that we were able to.

Jesus was very critical of the scribes and Pharisees, calling them hypocrites, because they tithed but neglected the more important matters — justice, mercy, and faith (see Matthew 23:23). Even though we do find that tithing (giving ten percent from the profits of land and livestock to the clergy for their support) was customary in Old Testament times, Jesus taught the Apostles to depend instead on charity when He sent them on their mission (see Matthew

10:9-10). St. Paul tells us that the Lord Himself "commanded that those who proclaim the gospel should get their living by the gospel" (1 Corinthians 9:14). Such support, of course, was spontaneous and within a person's means. In other words, Jesus was counting on the fact that any followers of His would always be moved by charity and give to support the Church in whatever way they could. Are we doing that?

The Catholic Church does not require a "tithe" of any percentage of income or any other source. As stated in the *Catechism of the Catholic Church* (n. 2043), the precepts of the Church maintain that "the faithful also have the duty of providing for the material needs of the Church, each according to his abilities [cf. CIC, can. 222]." Jesus said that a man cannot have two masters, God and money. The Church never demands that we give more than we can afford, but the truth is that many of us can afford to give more than we do. It is funny how, to so many, a hundred-dollar bill "looks" like so much when you take it to church but so little when you take it to the mall.

Dear Grace,

Is it a mortal sin to miss Mass on Sunday or holy days of obligation?

Yes, it is, if certain conditions are met. We commit mortal sin when the action is grave, or serious, and we do it on purpose, knowing that it is wrong in God's eyes. This question, however, often implies a lack of understanding of the communal nature of our faith. Mortal sin breaks our communion not only with God but also wounds our communion with the community of believers, our brothers and sisters in Christ. Jesus established a Church because He knew that we would need one another on our journey toward the Father. In the Mass, we receive the Eucharist, the sacrament of unity. By partaking of the one bread, we become one Body in Christ. We are not alone and what a more wonderful way to realize this than by worshipping our Lord together.

It is a serious sin to miss Mass deliberately. Not only did God say in the Ten Commandments, "You shall keep holy the Lord's Day," but Jesus also asked us at His Last Supper to "do this in remembrance of me" (Luke 22:19). The Mass is the memorial of Jesus' death and Resurrection. If we say we love Him, how can we stay away? Even though He was innocent, He willingly gave up His life on the cross so that we might have life. If He had not done that, there would have been no way for us to reach heaven.

Sometimes, it seems we forget that we, as human persons, are a unity of body and soul. We must, therefore, take care of the body and the spiritual part of us. If someone were to tell us that from this day forward, we would only be allowed to eat one meal a week, most of us would probably panic thinking that we might starve without food. And yet, that is exactly what we sometimes do to ourselves, because the Eucharist is the "food" that we need in order to live the Christian life and attain our eternal salvation. When we miss this meal, we are depriving ourselves of what we so desperately need.

If there is a good reason to miss Mass, it can be made up by going on another day of the week or saying prayers and meditating on the Scriptures for a period of time on that Sunday. Thus, missing Mass when we have a good reason is not considered mortal sin. However, we should always remember that we are the Body of Christ, which means that we not only have communion with Christ (the Head of the Body) but with the members — our brothers and sisters in Christ — as well. When we miss Mass, we miss in the sharing of that beautiful communion.

Dear Grace,

If a person commits suicide, will he or she be able to go to heaven?

This is most definitely a very difficult question because the situations when this happens may vary. Scripture tells us that we are made in the very image and likeness of God. Therefore, our life is sacred; it does not belong to us but to Him who gave it. It is a grave offense against God to take one's own life, especially when it is done deliberately. Sadly, however, suicide more often occurs when the persons are suffering from grave psychological disturbances or fear. Certainly, this would reduce or eliminate their responsibility before God.

The *Catechism of the Catholic Church* (n. 2283) states it very well: "We should not despair of the eternal salvation of persons who have taken their own lives. By ways known to him alone, God can provide the opportunity for salutary repentance. The Church prays for persons who have taken their own lives."

Dear Grace,

My wife and I have a question for you. Last week at Mass, our priest told us that people who have a maid working in their home should be paying her minimum wage. He says that this is what the Holy Father wants. Is this true? The girl we have working here is illegal. At least we are giving her a place to stay as well as some money to send to her family.

Some of the Holy Father's statements regarding human work can be found in his 1981 encyclical *Laborem Exercens*. In this important document, he states that "the Church considers it her task always to call attention to the dignity and rights of those who work [and] to condemn situations in which that dignity and those rights are violated." He tells us that not only are we to be concerned for providing employment for all workers but that we also have a moral duty to see to it that a "just remuneration" be given for work done.

He goes on to say that "in every system . . . wages . . . are still a *practical means* whereby the vast majority of people can have access to those goods which are intended for common use: both the goods of nature and manufactured goods. Both kinds of goods become accessible to the worker through the wage which he receives as remuneration for his work. Hence, in every case, a just wage is the concrete means of *verifying the justice* of the whole socioeconomic system and, in any case, of checking that it is functioning justly." This idea of checking to make sure that a worker is being paid justly concerns, above all, the family. Just remuneration for the work of an adult who is responsible for a family means remuneration that will suffice for establishing and properly maintaining a family and for providing security for its future.

Our Holy Father also addresses the issue of immigrants and their rights as workers. He writes that because it has resulted due to the complexities of modern life, "Man has the right to leave his native land for various motives — and also the right to return — in order to seek better conditions of life in another country." He adds: "The most important thing is that the person working away from his native land, whether as a permanent emigrant or as a seasonal worker, should not be *placed at a disadvantage* in comparison with the other workers in that society in the matter of working rights. Emigration in search of work must in no way become an opportunity for financial or social exploitation. In regard to the work relationship, the same criteria should be applied to immigrant workers as to all other workers in the society concerned. The value of work should be measured by the same standard and not according to the difference in nationality, religion or race."

It is unfortunate that today there are many who find themselves in a situation where they feel they must work in this country illegally. In most cases, it is a matter of survival for them and their family. The question of whether or not to hire them is entirely another matter. They do work here, and that we know. While our laws regarding minimum wage for workers do not apply to illegal aliens, we do have a moral duty as Christians to be as fair as possible if we employ these persons, even in our home. Several factors, of course, have to be taken into account.

In your case, where the girl is working for you and living in your home, it seems appropriate that the room and board should count as part of her wages. As far as the rest of her salary, it would be difficult to say how much exactly. Remember, every human person is made in the image and likeness of God and has dignity. Ask yourself, "What would Jesus do in this situation?" The Church can teach, advise, and guide us in this matter, but, in the end, an individual must follow his or her own conscience. I hope this helps you. God bless you and thank you for writing.

Dear Grace,

What is the Catholic Church's teaching on masturbation? Is it viewed as a mortal sin or as a venial sin? Could it prevent us from getting into heaven?

To answer this, let us look, first of all, at the Church's teaching. In 1975, the Congregation for the Doctrine of the Faith issued a *Declaration on Certain Problems of Sexual Ethics*, and it is this document that the *Catechism of the Catholic Church* quotes regarding this issue. " 'Both the Magisterium of the Church, in the course of a constant tradition, and the moral sense of the faithful have been in no doubt and have firmly maintained that masturbation is an intrinsically and gravely disordered action' [CDF, *Persona humana* 9]" (CCC, n. 2352). Whatever the motive, solitary sex in itself contradicts the meaning of human sexuality, which is meant by God to be shared between a man and a woman in marriage.

You ask if masturbation is viewed as a mortal or venial sin. Remember, that for a sin to be mortal, three conditions must together be met. It has to be a very serious and grave matter, which is committed with full knowledge and with deliberate consent. What we are saying is that for it to be mortal sin, it would have to be done deliberately, knowing that it is not what God wishes for us and without any regard for that. In order to judge the morality of a human act, certain conditions have to be considered. The Church recognizes, for example, that in the practice of masturbation, psychological factors including adolescent immaturity, lack of psychological balance, and even ingrained habit can influence a person's behavior, and this could lessen or even eliminate moral responsibility.

The condition that many persons claim for their innocence regarding masturbation is habit, and we certainly know how difficult habits are to break. We must keep in mind, however, that habit does not completely destroy the voluntary nature of our acts. As Christians who are going to be held accountable for our actions, we must strive to unite ourselves to the Lord and therefore do all we can to curb or eliminate all habits that detach us from Him.

The best thing a person can do if he or she is in doubt about the morality of any sexual activity is to talk to his or her confessor, a priest. After listening to all of the circumstances and conditions surrounding an individual's actions, he will make a judgment and give the proper guidance. Sometimes, professional help will have to be sought. But we should be careful with this because some professionals will actually encourage masturbation and this would be wrong. God knows that we will sometimes fail, but He does expect us to do our best to live according to His ways. He knows when we have done all we can to resist sin. If we have done that, then we can rest in the knowledge that we will enjoy a glorious happiness with Him in heaven one day.

Dear Grace,

In one of the Ten Commandments, we are told to keep holy the Sabbath. Does this mean that it is considered sinful to work on Sundays?

The Bible tells us that "in six days the LORD made heaven and earth, the sea, and all that is in them, and rested the seventh day; therefore the LORD blessed the sabbath day and hallowed it" (Exodus 20:11). For the Jewish people, the seventh day (or Sabbath) was always a "day of solemn rest, a holy sabbath to the LORD" (Exodus 16:23). They observed very strict rules about this day with no work of any kind permitted, and willful violation of the Sabbath was punishable with death.

Jesus was a Jew. Therefore, He observed the Sabbath, but He also ushered in a new understanding of it. He criticized the scribes and Pharisees for putting an intolerable burden on men's shoulders (see Matthew 23:4) and proclaimed that "the sabbath was made for man, not man for the sabbath; so the Son of man is lord even of the sabbath" (Mark 2:27-28). So, He cured people on the Sabbath, and this was one reason why they plotted to kill Him. After Christ died, rose from the dead, and ascended to heaven, the Church (with the authority given by Him) wanted to be as faithful to Jesus as possible; so, after careful discernment, the Sabbath was eventually replaced by the Christians with the Lord's Day, and was changed from Saturday to Sunday. This was done because some of the major salvation events, including the Resurrection, had taken place on a Sunday.

Because we still consider that Sunday worship fulfills the moral command of the Old Covenant, it remains as a day dedicated to the worship of God and to rest. The *Catechism of the Catholic Church* (n. 2185) states: "On Sundays and other holy days of obligation, the faithful are to refrain from engaging in work or activities that hinder the worship owed to God, the joy proper to the Lord's Day, the performance of the works of mercy, and the appropriate relaxation of mind and body [cf. CIC, can. 1247]. Family needs or important social service can legitimately excuse from the obligation of Sunday rest. The faithful should see to it that legitimate excuses do not lead to habits prejudicial to religion, family life, and health."

Today, many people have jobs that require them to work on Sunday. The Church would never say that we should leave our Sunday jobs if that is the best we can do. As Christians, however, we should always be striving to obtain employment that does not require Sunday work. In other words, it would only be sinful when or if we have made no effort to seek work that would allow us to be free on Sunday. In reality, any kind of labor that can be done on another day of the week and that might take us away from our focus on God, family, or charitable works is not good. All the other days of the week God allows for other things, but Sunday is a day for Him, a holy and sacred day.

Dear Grace,

Is it a sin to fantasize sexually, especially with someone in mind?

The Church teaches that "*lust* is disordered desire for or inordinate enjoyment of sexual pleasure." It is morally disordered when it is sought for itself instead of its procreative and unitive purposes (see CCC, n. 2351). We are all called to chastity, no matter what state in life we find ourselves in. In God's plan, sex and sexual pleasure are meant for marriage alone and to be enjoyed only in connection with God's purpose for sex and sexual pleasure. Sexual fantasies, if they are entertained for their own sake and as an end in themselves, can be sinful if they are voluntary. Sexual fantasies concerning one's spouse are a separate issue. They are not sinful when they conclude either in sexual union with one's spouse or are a byproduct of that union. This is so because under these conditions they occur within the context of marriage. Their end would be marital in this case, since they would not be sought for their own sake or as an end in themselves.

Yes, it is true that thoughts seem to work themselves into our minds almost without our willing them. God knows and understands our weaknesses. This does not excuse us, however, from an obligation to fight or resist them. It does not come easy, and it takes a lot of prayer and effort sometimes. Of course, there are many different circumstances, but if we are speaking about a person with no serious psychological disorder, then the act of fantasizing sexually without any effort to resist would be sinful.

Dear Grace,

Can a person who is a supporter of abortion receive Holy Communion?

This can be a very difficult question to answer because it asks about a "supporter" of abortion uniting himself to the Lord in Holy Communion. It can be confusing as to what *kind* of support is meant.

At the same time, it is a good question, for it should call each and every one of us to examine our own conscience regarding this absolutely critical issue, because one day God will hold us accountable for our actions. Therefore, let us be clear as to what the Church, in the name of God, teaches about what our stance should be regarding abortion.

In 1996, the National Conference of Catholic Bishops approved the following guidelines on the reception of Communion: "In order to be properly disposed to receive Communion, participants should not be conscious of grave sin and normally should have fasted for one hour. A person who is conscious of grave sin is not to receive the Body and Blood of the Lord without prior sacramental confession except for a grave reason where there is no opportunity for confession. In this case, the person is to be mindful of the obligation to make an act of perfect contrition, including the intention of confessing as soon as possible" (canon 916).

"Formal cooperation in an abortion constitutes a grave offense. The Church attaches the canonical penalty of excommunication to this crime against human life. 'A person who procures a completed abortion incurs excommunication . . .' [CIC, can. 1398] 'by the very commission of the offense' [CIC, can. 1314], and subject to the conditions provided by Canon Law [cf. CIC, cann. 1323-1324]" (CCC, n. 2272). In other words, according to canon law, the person must have had an abortion or directly participated in one in some way (like helping someone to get one) to be prevented from receiving Holy Communion. This excommunication is something that the person would bring on him- or herself as a result of his or her action.

We know clearly that abortion is the deliberate and intentional killing of an innocent, unborn child. The fact that the child is in the fetal stage of life does not in any way lessen or take away his right to life as a human person made in the image and likeness of God. It has always been the teaching of the Catholic Church that " 'God alone is the Lord of life from its beginning until its end: no one can under any circumstance claim for himself the right directly to destroy an innocent human being' [CDF, instruction, *Donum vitae*, intro. 5]" (CCC, n. 2258).

There are those who might say, "I support a woman's right to choose abortion, but I would never have one myself." The reality that they do not see is that to "support" abortion usually means that one aids directly or indirectly in making abortion more possible. If the person is being verbal in his support of abortion, he runs the risk of being guilty of the sin of scandal — an attitude or behavior that leads another to do evil. "Scandal is a grave offense if by deed or omission another is deliberately led into a grave offense" (CCC, n. 2284). Jesus Himself warned, "Whoever causes one of these little ones who believe in me to sin, it would be better for him to have a great millstone fastened round his neck and to be drowned in the depth of the sea. Woe to the world for temptations to sin! For it is necessary that temptations come, but woe to the man by whom the temptation comes!" (Matthew 18:6-7).

The Catholic bishops of the United States in their 1999 document "Faithful Citizenship" wrote the following: "Every human person is created in the image and likeness of God. The conviction that human life is sacred and that each person has inherent dignity that must be respected in society lies at the heart of Catholic social teaching. Calls to advance human rights are illusions if the right to life itself is subject to attack. We believe that every human life is sacred from conception to natural death; that people are more important than things; and that the measure of every institution is whether or not it enhances the life and dignity of the human person." Hence, as individuals we must examine our conscience in regard to this issue and where we stand.

Some will undoubtedly claim ignorance later by saying, "I didn't know." This is why we must teach, because even our ignorance will be accountable before God, especially when we had the means to know but chose not to. We must always remember, of course, that God is infinitely merciful to those who seek His forgiveness in a true and sincere way, and He is always ready to welcome us back with open arms to feast at His table. Yes, abortion is a forgivable sin, but we must first ask for that forgiveness. We should pray daily for the hardened hearts and clouded minds that some have regarding the killing of innocent, unborn children. Even from the cross, our Savior said, "Father, forgive them; for they know not what they do" (Luke 23:34).

Dear Grace,

Can I become a member of the Catholic Church if I support the death penalty?

The answer is yes, but you need to be aware that the Church supports it only in cases of absolute necessity. Let us consider the issue more closely. To be a member of the Catholic Church is, above all, to be a follower of Jesus Christ. In the one prayer that He gave us — the Lord's Prayer — He asked us to say, "And forgive us our debts, / As we also have forgiven our debtors" (Matthew 6:12; see also Luke 11:4). He must have known how difficult it would be for us to forgive those who hurt us or others. Capital punishment is a very painful issue, especially for the families of the victims of horrible crimes. However, because every human person is made in the image and likeness of God, the Catholic Church believes that she is called by Him to defend life whenever possible.

We read in the Old Testament that when Cain killed his brother, Abel, God (who is always merciful, even when He punishes) "put a mark on Cain, lest any who came upon him should kill him" (Genesis 4:15). He thus gave him a distinctive sign, not to condemn him to the hatred of others, but to protect and defend him from those wishing to kill him out of a desire to avenge Abel's death. Not even a murderer loses his personal dignity, and God himself pledges to guarantee this. It is precisely here that the paradoxical mystery of the merciful justice of God is shown forth (see *Evangelium Vitae*, Chap. 1).

On January 27, 1999, in St. Louis, Missouri, our Holy Father Pope John Paul II stated, "The new evangelization calls for followers of Christ, who are unconditionally pro-life, to proclaim, celebrate and serve the Gospel of life in every situation. A sign of hope is the increasing recognition that the dignity of human life must never be taken away, even in the case of someone who has done great evil. Modern society has the means of protecting itself, without definitively denying criminals the chance to reform. I renew the appeal I made most recently for a consensus to end the death penalty, which is both cruel and unnecessary." For more than twenty-five years, the Catholic bishops of the United States have also called for an end to the death penalty in our country.

The traditional teaching of the Church does not exclude recourse to the death penalty when this is the only practicable way to effectively defend the lives of human beings against the aggressor. If bloodless means are sufficient to protect the safety of persons, public authority should limit itself to such means. The Church also believes that today cases of absolute necessity for execution of the offender are very rare, if not practically nonexistent (see CCC, n. 2267).

Jesus said that we should love our enemies and do good to those who hate us. What a tall order that seems to be at times. The world is constantly telling us something else. The important thing to remember in this issue is that every human person has dignity. We are all loved by God, even the most hardened criminals. And yes, sometimes we may feel that God is asking too much of us to love those who have done us so much harm. We may think we cannot do that, but we must never forget that with God all things are possible.

While it is true that we must protect others and ourselves from those who would harm us, killing them is not the answer, except when it is the only way. The unwillingness to forgive is at the root of much evil in the world. We can change that. It must begin in the heart of every individual person.

Dear Grace,

Could you please explain why the Church teaches that having sex before marriage is wrong? What is the basis for this teaching?

With the authority given to her by God in Jesus Christ, the Catholic Church has, from the beginning, taught consistently that sexual intercourse "must take place exclusively within marriage. Outside of marriage it always constitutes a grave sin and excludes one from sacramental communion" (CCC, n. 2390). This teaching we firmly believe comes to us from God, and the Church cannot fail in her responsibility to proclaim this truth. Truth is not something subjective that one accepts only when it feels right or happens to fit our lifestyle. The truth is objective, and it changes for no one.

It is clear from Scripture that God intended for the sexual union between a man and a woman to be total and self-giving: "God blessed them, and God said to them, 'Be fruitful and multiply' " (Genesis 1:28). He made man and woman for each other and created marriage as the bond that would solidify and protect that union and, thus, the human family. God's plan was that the sexual act be open to life; this is part of marriage, and it is holy and honorable. Generally speaking, a couple with no permanent commitment to each other will not wish their sexual act to be open to life because of the possibility of children, who they may not be committed to raise and care for. Thus, they go against the plan of God when they have sex outside of marriage.

There are people today who would like to have a right to a "trial marriage" where there is an intention of getting married later. No matter how firm the purpose of those who engage in premature sexual relations may be, however, "carnal union is morally legitimate only when a definitive community of life between a man and woman has been established. Human love does not tolerate 'trial marriages.' It demands a total and definite gift of persons to one another [cf. FC 80]" (CCC, n. 2391).

In his apostolic exhortation *Familiaris Consortio* ("The Role of the Christian Family in the Modern World"), John Paul II has provided a clear and powerful summary of the Church's teaching on this matter. He states that sexuality is by no means something purely biological but concerns the innermost being of the human person. This total self-giving would be a lie if it were not the sign and fruit of a total, personal self-giving. If the person were to withhold something, then by this very fact he or she would not be giving totally.

We know, of course, that when nonmarried persons engage in sexual acts, there is often no thought given to this total gift of self. Pleasure and self-gratification are at times the motivating force. Every baptized person, however, is called to lead a chaste life in whatever state in life the person has chosen. In order to be chaste, one must learn self-control. It is when we can do this that we become truly free. We become who we really are, sons and daughters of the living God. We do not belong to ourselves, but to Him who made us out of love.

The Church is often challenged on this issue of no sex before marriage, but that can never change the truth that must be taught. Jesus, too, was often challenged, but if He had backed down, then He would not have been crucified and we would not have gained our eternal salvation. Many will ask how it can be wrong when so many are engaging in it. But thousands of wrongs do not make something right. Let us continue to pray to God for the grace and strength to do His will in our lives always.

Dear Grace,

I know that the Catholic Church teaches that artificial contraception is wrong but that natural family planning is acceptable. I do not understand how these two are so different that the Church approves one and not the other. Are they not, in reality, both a form of birth control?

This is an issue that many Catholics as well as non-Catholics struggle with, so it is very important to be clear on what the Church does indeed teach. First, let us define the terms. Artificial contraception is the intentional prevention of conception or impregnation through the use of various devices, agents, drugs, sexual practices, or surgical procedures before, during, or after a voluntary act of intercourse. Natural Family Planning (NFP), on the other hand, is a scientific method involving systematic observation of a woman's bodily signs of fertility and infertility through daily changes in body temperature and cervical mucus. All of these signs are carefully charted and studied to determine a woman's fertile period, and, on those days, the couple would have no sexual intercourse. Thus, normally no pregnancy would occur. This is not, by the way, the old "rhythm method" that is often confused with NFP. Another thing to keep in mind about NFP is that it is often used quite successfully to achieve pregnancy too.

Without careful consideration, one might conclude that artificial contraception and NFP amount to the same thing, since both appear to be an attempt to prevent pregnancy. To the world, this may be so, but in the eyes of God and of the Church they are very different, in the moral sense. What do we mean by that? Scripture tells us that God, out of His infinite and powerful love, created man and woman for each other. He then said to them, "Be fruitful and multiply, and fill the earth and subdue it" (Genesis 1:28). Even after they fell from His grace, He did not destroy them, but rather He continued to love them and immediately made a way for them and all their descendants to find their way back to Him. Here we see the creation and plan of God for marriage.

It is precisely because of the testimony of Scripture and the teachings of Jesus Christ that have been handed down to us by the Apostles (Tradition) that the Catholic Church has always and consistently taught that each and every marital act must remain open to the transmission of life. This is not something that the Church invented. It has come to us from God. He made marriage for two purposes: first, to be unitive — uniting the spouses in love; second, to be procreative — to bear children, if and when it was His divine will. These two purposes are inseparably connected in marriage, and man and woman must do nothing to break this connection, for to do so, would go directly contrary to the plan of the God (see CCC, n. 2366).

Knowing that God wills that every marital act of intercourse be open to the possibility of life, we can see that Natural Family Planning, if practiced for serious reasons, would not violate the natural law of God because with NFP there is no intercourse at all. Instead, there is abstinence — the man and woman say no to their own desires. With artificial contraception, however, there is sex with little or no possibility of life. Thus, artificial contraception is always wrong because it violates both the unitive and procreative purposes of marriage, whereas it is different with NFP when used in serious circumstances.

Sex is a beautiful and holy gift from God. Therefore, the husband and wife, under normal conditions, should not deprive each other. However, there may be times in their married life when a pregnancy would cause an undue hardship for either of the spouses or the family. In that case, NFP would be a possibility. Is the intention to cooperate with God's plan or to go against it? By practicing artificial contraception, knowing that it is contrary to God's plan for marriage, the couple is essentially saying, "We want this and it does not matter what God wants." This is so because, in this case, they have sex but say no to life.

Science teaches us that normally there are only a few days in a month when a woman may conceive a child. Even knowing this, many couples feel they cannot handle that. Yet, there can occur many times in a marriage when they must abstain from sex for a variety of reasons. This is truly something to think about. The beautiful mystery is that in doing His will and living the life He meant for us, it will always and forever be where our true happiness and fulfillment will be found.

Dear Grace,

You have said that God made marriage for two inseparable purposes: (1) to unite the spouses in love; (2) to engage in intercourse only with the possibility of conception. Based upon that premise: (1) intercourse using NFP, knowing that there will be no conception, satisfies the natural law of God; (2)

intercourse using artificial contraception, knowing that there will be no conception, does not satisfy the natural law of God. Is my understanding correct?

On a basic level, your understanding is correct, but it needs some clarification. First, allow me to repeat that the two purposes of marriage — to be unitive and procreative — are inseparably connected in marriage, and man and woman must do nothing to break this connection (see CCC, n. 2366). How is this connected to the natural law?

If we accept that God has a plan of salvation for all mankind, then it makes logical sense that when He creates every human person, He instills in that person all that is necessary to attain that salvation. Each one of us is on a journey back to the One who created us. That is our eternal destiny. On this journey, however, we have the freedom to make the choices in our lives that will lead us either away or toward that destiny. Thus, deep within, God instills in us what is called the natural law.

In his encyclical *Veritatis Splendor* ("The Splendor of Truth," n. 54), John Paul II quotes from the Second Vatican Council and Scripture: "In the depths of his conscience man detects a law which he does not impose on himself, but which holds him to obedience. . . . For man has in his heart a law written by God. To obey it is the very dignity of man; according to it he will be judged (cf. *Rom* 2:14-16)."

Your understanding of the difference between the use of artificial contraception and Natural Family Planning is technically correct, but the words used are not exactly the best. You speak in terms of two ways to have intercourse, one that "satisfies" the natural law of God and one that does not. Rather than use the word "satisfies," it might be better to think in terms of listening to and obeying that "light of understanding infused in us by God, whereby we understand what must be done and what must be avoided" (*Veritatis Splendor*, n. 12).

When a couple practices NFP, they will not have intercourse during fertile periods, unless, of course, they are infertile and are using NFP as a method to help them conceive a child. But when the purpose is to not conceive and they are using NFP, then when they do have sex, it will unite them in love by bringing them closer together because every marital act will be open to life. In other words, it will not separate the two purposes of God for marriage. If they use artificial birth control, however, they will have intercourse, but the two purposes of marriage will be separated because their act will not be open to life and also because what should be a total gift of self will be a lie. They are not giving themselves totally, but instead they are holding something back.

One more thing to keep in mind is that NFP is not to be practiced for the sake of convenience. For example, it would not be morally in accordance with the natural law for couples to decide to practice NFP because they want to take a vacation this year or some other similar reason. This is one very crucial reason why couples need to think and consider well if they are indeed prepared for the responsibilities of marriage before entering into this covenant with each other and God.

No matter what the world tells us, sex was not made for self-gratification or simply to make a partner "feel good." God made it for the sharing of love and the transmission of life. This is the natural law written in the hearts of men and women.

Dear Grace,

I understand that lying is wrong, but is it always wrong? Are there not situations when it would be permissible?

Lying is indeed a very serious matter, and many do not even realize how serious it is. The *Catechism of the Catholic Church* (n. 2482) quotes St. Augustine's teaching that "a *lie* consists in speaking a falsehood with the intention of deceiving." The Eighth Commandment forbids misrepresenting the truth in our relations with others. This is because God, who is the Truth, calls us to live in truth.

The *Catechism* (n. 2484) goes on to say that "the *gravity of a lie* is measured against the nature of the truth it deforms, the circumstances, the intentions of the one who lies, and the harm suffered by its victims. To lie is to speak or act against the truth in order to lead someone into error." We can see, therefore, that every case must be considered and evaluated individually. We would do this in order to decide how grave the sin of the lie is, rather than to decide if the lie was itself good, because lying is never in itself a good thing.

Is it the same when you tell your friend that you like her new hairdo when in reality you do not, as when you tell your husband or wife that you were working late, when in reality you were out with someone else? In both cases, one might claim to be lying in order not to hurt the other person. The Church tells us that "by its very nature, lying is to be condemned. . . . The culpability is greater when the intention of deceiving entails the risk of deadly consequences for those who are led astray" (CCC, n. 2485).

So, lying is never really good, but let us say that there may be certain situations when it would be morally permissible to withhold the truth. "The good and safety of others, respect for privacy, and the common good are sufficient reasons for being silent about what ought not be known or for making use of a discreet language. . . . No one is bound to reveal the truth to someone who does not have the right to know it [cf. *Sir* 27:16; *Prov* 25:9-10]" (CCC, n. 2489). In other words, sometimes people do not have the right to know the truth, such as when someone asks you questions about your personal life and he or she has no need to know. In such a case, you are not bound to reveal the truth to such people.

Sadly, today lying has become so habitual that people do not even seem to know the difference anymore. Children lie to their parents, spouses lie to each other, people lie on their tax forms and applications, and the list goes on and on. If we were to sit and meditate on it deeply, we would realize that in every situation where there is lying, something is always wrong. Sin is always at the root of every lie, even the most seemingly innocent ones. Why is it that Jesus called the devil "a liar and the father of lies" (John 8:44)?

One way to avoid the sin of lying is to pray and ask God for His help and merciful guidance. We cannot do it alone. If we are sincere and ready to do all we can to change and live a life of truth as He wishes for us, He will grant to us the strength and grace to be victorious in overcoming this temptation. It is always a wonderful thing to know a truthful person. Telling the truth is a great witness to the Christian faith.

Dear Grace,

I have a friend who is Catholic and she has had an abortion. I love her dearly and have become so afraid and anxious for her soul. Will she go to hell? Will God forgive this sin? Will she be punished for the rest of her life?

In answering this, I am assuming that you are referring to a direct abortion, which is the deliberate and intentional killing of an unborn baby in the womb, because that is precisely what abortion is. Without question, this is one of the gravest moral issues facing us today.

The Catholic Church has always taught that "*human life is sacred* because from its beginning it involves the creative action of God and it remains for ever in a special relationship with the Creator, who is its sole end. God alone is the Lord of life from its beginning until its end: no one can under any circumstance claim for himself the right directly to destroy an innocent human being" (Congregation for the Doctrine of the Faith, instruction, *Donum vitae*, intro. 5).

From the advances in science, we now know that a baby's life does not begin on the day of birth, but rather at conception. This is what makes abortion, when it is done with full knowledge and intention, a mortal sin — taking the life of an innocent human being. Why do people have a hard time seeing this? It seems that today so much of the world is in some sort of blindness about the gravity of abortion. Ask yourself the following, however: How many people could kill a live baby if you placed the infant in front of them and asked, "Can you kill your child now?" I doubt that many could or would do such a thing. Then why is abortion acceptable?

We know, of course, that there exist many circumstances surrounding every kind of sin, and this is certainly true about abortion. Sometimes fear, pressure, shame, or ignorance can lead a person to make horrible mistakes or take the most unspeakable actions. The thing to remember always is that God sees our heart, soul, and mind. He knows if we are innocent or guilty. Reminding us of the Fifth Commandment, Jesus said, "You shall not kill; and whoever kills shall be liable to judgment" (Matthew 5:21).

When we commit a mortal sin, by our own action we have cut ourselves off from God. It is not God who turns away from us, but we who turn away from Him. You ask if your friend will go to hell or if God will forgive her. Everything we know about God tells us that He is a God of infinite love and mercy. He is also, however, a God of justice. We sometimes do not want to be reminded of that. Yes, God will forgive, but first your friend must ask for this forgiveness, and if the action was deliberate, then some reparation will have to be made. But you see, if she is truly and deeply sorry in her heart, then she will gladly and willingly want to do this.

We should not be anxious or fearful of going to hell. No one ends up in hell unless he chooses to go there. So many people are keeping themselves separated from the love and mercy of God because they say they fear He will not forgive them, but that is not true of God. Perhaps what they really fear is His demand for justice, not realizing that love, mercy, and justice go together. Sometimes there is a lack of desire to make the changes in one's life in order to turn away from sin. The very best you can do for your friend, if you are close enough to do so in a loving way, is to help her to come to the realization of the meaning of abortion. Then, guide and encourage her toward the sacrament of Reconciliation, where Jesus Christ is waiting to meet her with open arms.

Dear Grace,

Can a person who is Catholic, but not married in the Church, be a CCD teacher?

A person who is married outside of the Catholic Church is, by his or her very actions, not in full communion with the Church and therefore is not qualified to teach the Catholic faith to others. To teach the Catholic faith essentially means to teach Christ and all that He taught. As well-intending as the person may be, he must ask himself, "Is my life and the way I live a reflection of what Jesus taught? Am I a good example for children or young people of how they should live in Christ?" Although a person might say that he has no intention of sharing his personal life with his CCD students or to encourage them to live as he does, by his very example he does so.

In his apostolic exhortation *Catechesi Tradendae* ("Catechesis in Our Time"), our Holy Father John Paul II explains and makes clear for us the duties and responsibilities entrusted to the Church, by Christ Himself, to teach the Catholic faith. Jesus gave to the Apostles one final command — to make disciples of all the nations and to teach them to observe all that He had commanded (see Matthew 28:19-20).

A CCD teacher is called a catechist. What is "catechesis"? It is education in the faith for children, young people, and adults that includes especially the teaching of Christian doctrine and taught in a way that will help the one who hears it to enter fully into the Christian life (see *Catechesi Tradendae*, n. 18). In order to teach Christ, however, a catechist must first "put on" Christ — become like Him. It is Christ alone who teaches. Anyone teaches Him to the extent that he or she is Christ's spokesman, enabling Christ to teach with his or her lips. Every catechist must strive constantly to transmit by his or her teaching and behavior the teaching and life of Jesus (see *Catechesi Tradendae*, n. 6).

It can be a very painful situation for those who have separated themselves from some of the aspects of the Church's life and faith by stepping outside of it in the choices they have made. Sometimes it may happen that they took these actions not understanding the consequences. It is very evident that many people do not have a full knowledge of the faith, and this is not always through their own fault. This is a very serious matter and one that a person should consider carefully with thought of doing something about it.

The mistake that we often make is in thinking we have all the time in the world to change our ways and become what God wants for us. Satan convinces us of that. It is his great lie. One day, though, all of the tomorrows we thought we had will be gone, and we will be face to face with Jesus. Every action in this life will have a consequence. So, if a person is not living according to our Lord's teachings, he or she should do something about it today. If you are married outside the Church, it may be possible to have your marriage validated so that you may be in full communion again. Talk to your pastor and seek the help of the Church. It is your home, where you belong.

Dear Grace,

I am confused about something. If the Church teaches that we should follow our conscience, but then turns around and teaches us that we must obey Church teaching, then what is the difference? Who am I supposed to follow, the Church's teaching or my own conscience? How will I know what is the right thing to do?

Yes, it is true that the Church teaches that no person must be forced to act contrary to his or her conscience. Nor must he or she be prevented from acting according to his or her conscience, especially in religious matters (see *Dignitatis Humanae*). The reason that the Church can teach this, however, is because she knows that "deep within his conscience man discovers a law which he has not laid upon himself but which he must obey. Its voice, ever calling him to love and to do what is good and to avoid evil, sounds in his heart at the right moment. . . . For man has in his heart a law inscribed by God. . . . His conscience is man's most secret core and his sanctuary. There he is alone with God whose voice echoes in his depths" (*Gaudium et Spes, n.* 16).

What the Church is telling us is that when we truly listen to our conscience, we will hear God speaking to us. We were created by God. He made us and we are on a journey back to Him. He wants us to be very happy, and because He made us He knows best all that is good for us. So, He instills inside of us this conscience through which He will try to guide and lead us to do what is good and right.

In this life, we will face many serious moral decisions, and we will have choices to make. These choices cannot be made blindly. In other words, our conscience must be informed. This means that we must first take certain steps to learn everything we can in regard to what we are trying to make a decision about. This can be referred to as discernment.

Let us say that you are a parent, and your son or daughter has come to you and asked you to help him or her to have an abortion. This would certainly be a grave moral decision requiring the formation of conscience. What do you do? The first thing to do is to listen to what the Church has to say on the matter and why. Remember that the Church was established by Jesus Christ, who was God Himself, and given authority by Him to teach in His name. So, when we listen to the Church, we hear God. In a case as grave as abortion, what the Church teaches should be what we follow because she speaks for God and teaches infallibly in matters of faith and morals.

In making decisions or choices that are less grave, there are additional steps we can take to inform our conscience in order to do what is right before God. We should consult professionals and get expert advice. Find out what is involved in any procedures that will be required. Then, seek advice from trusted friends and family or anyone who might have gone through the same experience. Finally, take the matter before the Lord in prayer, asking Him to reveal to you, through your conscience, what you should do.

When you have done all these things, make your decision, and move forward. This way, even if you make a mistake, you will be able to say to God that you did all you could. You did your best. He knows our hearts and minds and will know if we are sincere. You see, the Church can say, "Follow your conscience," because she knows that if you truly listen to God in your conscience, then what you hear will be no different from what the Church teaches, for she teaches only what God has revealed to her. Thus, there is no conflict between following your conscience and following the Church.

Dear Grace,

If you do not agree with some of the Church's teachings, but you receive Communion on Sundays, are you sinning?

First of all, let us be clear that "not agreeing with" and "not living according to" the Church's teachings are two different matters. It is very possible that a person might not agree with a teaching and yet decide to live in obedience to it, believing that it comes from God. The Church knows well that sometimes we will struggle with a certain teaching, often due to a lack of understanding, and this is okay as long as we do not reject it. If, however, you are asking if it is all right to receive Holy Communion and, at the same time, live a life that rejects some of the teachings of the Church, the answer depends on what teachings you are referring to. Certain "teachings," or doctrines, of the Church must be believed and followed, otherwise communion with the Church and with God would be broken.

What are those teachings that must be believed and followed? Canon law states the following: "All that is contained in the written Word of God or in Tradition, that is, in the one deposit of faith entrusted to the Church and also proposed as divinely revealed either by the solemn Magisterium of the Church or by its ordinary and universal Magisterium, must be believed with divine and catholic faith. . . . Therefore, all are bound to avoid any doctrines whatever which are contrary to these truths" (canon 750). This means everything that has been revealed by God to the Church, both written and oral. By "Magisterium," we mean the teaching office of the Church. As has been pointed out before, it is made up of the pope and bishops. When they together teach in an area pertaining to faith and morals, they are the Magisterium.

We know that essentially any baptized Catholic, unless prohibited by canon law, may be admitted to Holy Communion (see canon 912). In other words, one may receive Communion as long as one is not acting contrary to any law of the Church. We must keep in mind, of course, that when we speak here of the "laws" of the Church, we are speaking of the law of God, and most of it is based on the Ten Commandments, which are to us like signposts on the road to life. God reveals them to us out of His great love and infinite mercy. Who knows better what we need than He who made us?

Sometimes we may tend to think that by the Ten Commandments God means to bind or limit us, when in fact just the opposite is true. In actuality, they are meant to liberate us, to set us free. The problem with embracing them comes when we do not want to accept no for an answer to what we want. When as children, however, we wanted to play with matches or a knife and our parents said no, we did not understand then what we do now as adults about the danger in having such things. It is that same way, too, between God and us.

So, when God tells us that those things such as abortion, sex outside of marriage, marriage outside the Church, artificial birth control, practicing homosexuality, "living together," are wrong, then we know they are not His divine will for us. If we disobey deliberately and willingly, then we have fallen out of communion with Him. This is mortal sin and therefore one may not receive the Holy Eucharist while the situation persists. Reconciliation, however, can restore that communion. If only we realized the great mercy of God. He waits lovingly and eagerly for each of us to reach out to Him and be with Him. To be in the will of the Lord and live according to His ways brings a happiness and peace that every human person was made for and longs for. Let us pray for this communion with Him for each other, today and every day.

Dear Grace,

Is it against the Church's belief to shop at the malls and grocery stores on Sunday?

Shopping at the malls and buying groceries on Sunday is certainly not what the Church ever intended for the Christian faithful. The Lord's Day, like the Jewish Sabbath, has always been meant to be a day dedicated to God, family, and rest. It is disappointing indeed to see the stores so filled on Sunday. God asks us to worship Him and to rest on that day. How amazing it is that we have gotten so far away from this!

The *Catechism of the Catholic Church* (n. 2185) states the following: "On Sundays and other holy days of obligation, the faithful are to refrain from engaging in work or activities that hinder the worship owed to God, the joy proper to the Lord's Day, the performance of the works of mercy, and the appropriate relaxation of mind and body [cf. CIC, can. 1247]. Family needs or important social service can legitimately excuse from the obligation of Sunday rest. The faithful should see to it that legitimate excuses do not lead to habits prejudicial to religion, family life, and health."

Some might ask, "Why are the malls and stores open on Sunday, then, if it is wrong to shop there?" What we should ask ourselves instead, however, is this: "Would the stores be open on Sunday if we were honoring God's Third Commandment to keep holy the Lord's Day?" The Scripture tells us that God created the heavens and the earth and then He rested from His work of creation (see Genesis 2:1-3). We are therefore called to rest from our labors as He did. "So then, there remains a sabbath rest for the people of God; for whoever enters God's rest also ceases from his labors as God did from his" (Hebrews 4:9-10).

"Those Christians who have leisure should be mindful of their brethren who have the same needs and the same rights, yet cannot rest from work because of poverty and misery. Sunday is traditionally consecrated by Christian piety to good works and humble service of the sick, the infirm, and the elderly. Christians will also sanctify Sunday by devoting time and care to their families and relatives, often difficult to do on other days of the week. Sunday is a time for reflection, silence, cultivation of the mind, and meditation which furthers the growth of the Christian interior life" (CCC, n. 2186).

Perhaps what we sometimes fail to consider is that when we choose to shop at the malls or other stores on Sunday, we make it necessary for those persons to work who may wish to be off on Sunday but who are required to work by their employers because so many people expect the malls to be open on Sunday. They cannot have the day off because people who want to shop on Sunday have made it profitable for stores to be open on that day. There was a time when this was not the case. We should pray for those who have to work on the Lord's Day, that one day they will no longer have to.

Often what is needed is a better scheduling and planning of our time so that on Sunday we can devote the day to God, our family, and rest. Of course, if there is a serious need to buy food or medicine on Sunday, then we must do so. We should, however, make every effort to buy these things on another day of the week if at all possible. God calls us to come closer to Him, and the Sunday rest is one of the best ways we can do this.

Probably the reason that this whole issue of shopping on Sunday is such a challenge for us is because it has become a habit, something we have become accustomed to. This is something to look at and consider carefully. When was the last time we started the day with Mass, prepared a delicious, wholesome meal for our family, played games with our children, visited an elderly relative who might be lonely, sat and read our Bible, or just spent some time talking to someone about God? These are the things our Sunday should be filled with, not shopping. Let us not treat it like any other day of the week. Sunday is to be set apart. It is different. It is special. It is the Lord's Day!

Dear Grace,

My son and I were discussing the importance of the Ten Commandments and how they are to be used as a guide. He says they are part of the Old Testament and therefore we need not focus that much on them. His attitude toward them is that they are just a lot of "Do Not's." Can you help me explain why God gave us these commandments and why they are still important for us today?

While it is certainly true that many people have this understanding or attitude toward the Ten Commandments, it just so happens that the complete opposite is true. The reality, you see, is that the reason God gave them to us was not to limit or restrict us but rather to set us free — free from sin. Who is it that knows us better than the One who made us? Because we belong to God who loves us so much, the only way we can be truly free and happy is when we live according to His ways. That is when we become "who we really are" — sons and daughters of the one, true, and living God. It is precisely when we try to be "who we are not" that we are not free.

Deep within every human heart, God instills what is known as the natural law, a sort of code of moral conduct by which our reason tells us whether something is in conformity with our true human nature (see Romans 2:15). All of those things that are not in agreement with our nature we are obviously to avoid because ultimately they will not fulfill us. In other words, they will hinder and possibly destroy the possibility of attaining our true destiny, heaven. This should make sense. Would we feed our bodies gasoline when they are made to live on food and water? This same basic principle applies to the moral order of our lives, for we are a people who are a unity of body and soul. The Ten Commandments are, if you will, a summary of this natural law, which reveals all that is good for us. When the Hebrews, wandering in the desert, failed to obey the natural law within them, God then gave to them the revealed law — the Ten Commandments.

In his beautiful encyclical *Veritatis Splendor* the Holy Father John Paul II tells us that man's freedom is not unlimited. Every human person "is called to accept the moral law given by God. In fact, human freedom finds its authentic and complete fulfillment precisely in the acceptance of that law. God, who alone is good, knows perfectly what is good for man, and by virtue of his very love proposes this good to man in the commandments. God's law does not reduce, much less do away with human freedom; rather, it protects and promotes that freedom" (n. 35).

Throughout the Scriptures, a certain theme is woven in — that in life, there are two roads, the road to life and the road to death. By this we mean eternal life and eternal death, for we know that our life on earth is temporary. If you can imagine this, on the road to life, there are "signposts," if you will, and these signposts are the Ten Commandments. This connection between the commandments and eternal life is clearly demonstrated by Jesus in the story of the rich young man in Matthew's Gospel. When asked, "Teacher, what good deed must I do, to have eternal life?" He answered him, "If you would enter life, keep the commandments" (Matthew 19:16-17).

Yes, to many the commandments seem so challenging and restrictive, and this is so because we live in a world where at every turn there is the temptation to sin. But, like Peter, who could do what seemed like the impossible when he walked on water only by keeping his eyes fixed on Jesus (see Matthew 14:29-30), we, too, can follow the Lord to our heavenly home. So, let us follow the "signs." The road to life is the right road to be on! You are indeed a good mother in wanting to teach your children to love God.

Dear Grace,

I know that the Catholic Church prohibits artificial birth control because it "goes against nature." What is the Church's position on Viagra? I think it goes against nature just as much as artificial birth control does.

As far as we know, the Church has not condemned the use of Viagra. Your question is interesting and occasions an opportunity to make an important distinction. Artificial contraception, as has been pointed out elsewhere in this book, is the intentional prevention of conception or impregnation through the use of various devices, agents, drugs, sexual practices, or surgical procedures before, during, or after a voluntary act of intercourse. Viagra, on the other hand, is a drug that helps males to overcome a pathological condition preventing them from engaging in the conjugal act with their spouses. Destroying or denying a good (conception) is quite different from enhancing or strengthening a good, by use of Viagra.

Is it wrong for a married man to be assisted by medical treatment to have sexual relations with his wife? Surely it cannot be. Scripture tells us that God, out of His infinite and powerful love, created man and woman for each other. He then said to them, "Be fruitful and multiply, and fill the earth and subdue it" (Genesis 1:28). God had a beautiful plan for marriage. And in order that men and women would be able to fulfill that plan, God created them with a natural desire for each other. This desire is good and noble when it is satisfied in the way that the Creator intended. Sex is a sacred and holy gift from God to a husband and wife because this is one of the means by which they can fulfill the two purposes and meanings of marriage — to be unitive and to be procreative. Let us not make the mistake, though, of placing all of the focus on sex. Sexual performance is not the end-all in marriage and really has little to do with the spiritual aspect of marriage.

Use of drugs such as Viagra to help overcome pathological conditions can certainly not be immoral. The difference between use of such drugs and artificial contraceptives is that contraceptives do not help overcome a pathological condition. Being fertile is not a pathology. There is quite a difference. Viagra does not go against nature — it assists nature. Artificial contraception does not assist nature — it goes against nature.

I assumed, of course, that you were referring to married men in your question. If, however, you were asking about all men using Viagra, then that would change the answer. The Catholic Church has always taught consistently that sexual intercourse "must take place exclusively within marriage. Outside of marriage it always constitutes grave sin and excludes one from sacramental communion" (CCC, n. 2390).

You can see, therefore, that because we believe firmly that sex outside of marriage is immoral, then the use of Viagra — a drug specifically used to assist males to be able to have sexual intercourse — would most naturally be condemned as immoral if used by single men. This teaching by the Church regarding no sex outside of marriage is often not a popular one and creates a tremendous challenge for many single persons today, but the reality is that it is a beautiful teaching, for it comes from God, and therefore we know that it comes from His loving heart and is thus for our ultimate good and true happiness.

Dear Grace,

When people are mentally ill and they do wrong things as a result of their psychosis, does God know that? Do people need to go to confession over what they do when they are not well? And do God and the Church understand the special needs and circumstances of the mentally ill?

Sacred Scripture begins with these solemn words, and this we believe: "In the beginning God created the heavens and the earth" (Genesis 1:1). In a way, this helps in answering part of your question, "Does God know, and does God understand?" Yes, indeed, as Creator of all, He knows and understands all. And this is also why God is the only one who can judge ultimately all of our actions. Who else can look inside our minds and hearts and see why we do the things we do? Most especially, He knows and understands those who are weak, ill, or suffering through no fault of their own.

Regarding Confession, you are asking essentially whether or not a person who is mentally ill is morally responsible for wrongs or sins committed as a direct result of his or her illness. No, such a person is not responsible and this is due to the fact that a person who is mentally ill is not acting with free choice. To understand this better we should first consider what sin is. In simple terms, sin is an offense against God, a turning away from Him and His love and, instead, deliberately choosing our own will over His. As the Psalmist cries out, "Against thee, thee only, have I sinned, / and done that which is evil in thy sight" (Psalm 51:4). Another thing we know about sin is that it is rooted in the heart of man, in his free will. Jesus said that it is from man's heart that evil comes (see Matthew 15:19-20). Thus, free choice must play a part in sin.

Let us repeat again the three conditions for mortal sin. The *Catechism of the Catholic Church* (n. 1857) states: " 'Mortal sin is sin whose object is grave matter and which is also committed with full knowledge and deliberate consent' [*RP* 17 § 12]." We note, then, that deliberate free will and knowledge play a crucial and essential role in determining moral responsibility for sinful actions or thoughts.

To demonstrate how the Church truly does understand the special needs and circumstances of the mentally ill, the *Catechism* continues its explanation of this issue in the following two paragraphs:

1859: Mortal sin requires *full knowledge* and *complete consent*. It presupposes knowledge of the sinful character of the act, of its opposition to God's law. It also implies a consent sufficiently deliberate to be a personal choice. Feigned ignorance and hardness of heart [cf. *Mk* 3:5-6; *Lk* 16:19-31] do not diminish, but rather increase, the voluntary character of a sin.

1860: *Unintentional ignorance* can diminish or even remove the imputability of a grave offense. But no one is deemed to be ignorant of the principles of the moral law, which are written in the conscience of every man. The promptings of feelings and passions can also diminish the voluntary and free character of the offense, as can external pressures or pathological disorders. Sin committed through malice, by deliberate choice of evil, is the gravest.

In other words, for Confession to be required (see canon 988), a person would have had to know fully that his or her action was an offense against God and then proceeded to do it anyway. There are certain conditions, however, that can impede this knowledge and free will. Mental illness, in most cases, constitutes such a condition because of the way that it can affect the operation of intellect and free choice. In some cases, though, it is extremely difficult to determine moral responsibility. These must be left in the hands of God, who always knows the human heart of the one who is innocent of wrongs committed. And, in addition, our faith leads us to say with all certainty that even in situations when a person is not innocent, God's mercy is infinite for the one who seeks Him.

Dear Grace,

I have a sister who is involved with a married man. As much as I am against it, is it a sin for me to listen to her talk to me of her involvement with this man? Is it also a sin for me to pray for her happiness if it means involvement with this man? I would certainly appreciate your input in this matter.

What a sad and difficult situation this must be for you. Adultery is a serious sin, a mortal sin, and you are right in being very concerned. Before we address your questions, let us first consider the gravity of your sister's actions. What is adultery? The *Catechism of the Catholic Church* (n. 2380) states the following: "*Adultery* refers to marital infidelity. When two partners, of whom at least one is married to another party, have sexual relations — even transient ones — they commit adultery."

It continues by stating, "Adultery is an injustice. He who commits adultery fails in his commitment. He does injury to the sign of the covenant which the marriage bond is, transgresses the rights of the other spouse, and undermines the institution of marriage by breaking the contract on which it is based. He compromises the good of human generation and the welfare of children who need their parents' stable union" (CCC, n. 2381).

Adultery was forbidden by God as one of the Ten Commandments — "You shall not commit adultery" (Exodus 20:14). Jesus also condemned it by teaching that not only is committing of the act sinful but so is the desire for it. His teaching was clear: "Every one who looks at a woman lustfully has already committed adultery with her in his heart" (Matthew 5:28).

Knowing then what injurious and grave sin adultery is, is it a sin for you to listen to your sister speak about her involvement with this man? The answer is that it depends on the circumstances. Perhaps your sister is really in need of someone to confide in and is subconsciously looking for someone to talk her out of it. Knowing that adultery is wrong and an offense against God, you have a moral obligation to try to help your sister to realize the error of her ways. This must be done with charity but also firmness and conviction. After all, she is your sister, not a stranger. You have a close relationship with her that allows the opportunity to speak to her about this. To say nothing would definitely be wrong. If you saw your sister about to jump off a cliff to her death, would you stand by and say, "It's none of my business"? Your sister is in a similar situation in that she is committing mortal sin and is in danger of spiritual death.

On the other hand, we must consider that this situation could possibly present an occasion of sin for you as well. However, because you say that you are very much against it, then it would not be as serious an occasion of sin for you as it might be for a person who perhaps has been guilty of such sin in the past. As Christians, we are under moral obligation to avoid all sin, but some situations make it very difficult for us, as with your listening to your sister speak about her adulterous relationship. Certainly it would be wrong for you to sit by and pretend that it is acceptable. You should pray to God for the strength and wisdom to know when to speak and what to say. He will help you.

It is possible too that, in being there for her, you will be able to lead her closer to God by your own good example of Christian living. Often, this can be the best witness. But never should you forget your duty as a follower of Christ to help a fellow brother or sister. When you ask if it is sinful to pray for her happiness even if it means involvement with this man, you must realize that her true happiness can never be with this man as long as he is married to another woman. Only when we follow and obey the law of God, which is based on His infinite love for us, can we be truly happy, fulfilled, and free. Speak to her often of God and His love for her. Jesus forgave the adulterous woman but then said, "Go, and do not sin again" (John 8:11).

Dear Grace,

My mom has advanced vascular dementia and is heavily medicated with anti-psychotics and sleeping pills. She lives in a drug-induced, sleeplike state, and this seems to be all there is left for her. She is on a large amount of drugs for heart failure, and it seems that her heart medications keep her body alive, while her mind is dying. I have prayed for three years for God to call her home or to grant her some type of mental peace and have asked her doctor (a devout Catholic) to stop the medications for her heart, but he says that would most likely be fatal for her. I am asking you if withholding medication and allowing a natural death to occur is the same as euthanasia. I don't know how to help my mother be freed from the awful mental state that now tortures her. Must we keep medicating and feeding her? Is it acceptable by Church law to stop her heart medications and let God maintain her body on earth or call her home? I do not want to offend God in any way and want to understand the Church's teaching.

I know you love your mother very much, and what a painful and difficult situation this must be for your whole family. Your willingness to follow God's law is also to be commended. Please keep in mind that in such grave moral matters every case must be considered individually. Readers are cautioned that this discussion may not apply to every circumstance and that they should speak to their pastor when they are in need of clarification and understanding of Church teaching. Having said that, let us speak of your particular situation. We will look first to the teaching of the Church, as found in the Congregation for the Doctrine of the Faith's 1980 *Declaration on Euthanasia*. Here is what it says:

"By euthanasia is understood an action *or an omission* which of itself or by intention causes death, in order that all suffering may in this way be eliminated. Euthanasia's terms of reference, therefore, are to be found in the intention of the will and in the methods used. It is necessary to state firmly once more that nothing and no one can in any way permit the killing of an innocent human being, whether a fetus or an embryo, an infant or an adult, an old person, or one suffering from an incurable disease, or a person who is dying. Furthermore, no one is permitted to ask for this act of killing, either for himself or herself or for another person entrusted to his or her care, nor can he or she consent to it, either explicitly or implicitly. nor can any authority legitimately recommend or permit such an action." [*Declaration on Euthanasia*, II; emphasis added]

From what you tell me, your mother is still very much alive. Even though her mind has deteriorated, she is not what would be referred to as "brain dead." If that were the case, the answer might be different. Regarding what you describe, however, it would be morally wrong to withhold medical treatment if this would certainly kill her. Taking her off of her heart medicine would constitute what Catholic moral theologian Dr. William E. May describes as " 'passive euthanasia' — in which someone brings about the death of a person for merciful reasons by an act of omission, i.e., by withholding or withdrawing medical treatments that could preserve that person's life, precisely to bring about death [in other words, 'allowing' the person to die a natural death]" (*Catholic Bioethics and the Gift of Human Life*, p. 239).

The Church makes it clear that gravely ill persons are to be assisted and cared for with Christian charity at the end of their life. Our Holy Father John Paul II reminds us that our culture today sometimes fails to perceive any meaning or value in suffering. Instead, it considers suffering as the epitome of evil, something to be eliminated at all costs. He states that this leads people to think that they can control life and death by taking the decisions about them into their own hands (see *Evangelium Vitae*, n. 15). "According to Christian teaching, however, suffering, especially suffering during the last moments of life, has a special place in God's saving plan; it is in fact a sharing in Christ's passion and a union with the redeeming sacrifice which He offered in obedience to the Father's will" (*Declaration on Euthanasia*, III).

Usually, what a person who is suffering needs more than anything is love and care. How wonderful and peaceful we feel when we know that someone loves us. The *Declaration on Euthanasia* concludes by pointing out that such service to people is also service to Christ the Lord, who said: "As you did it to one of the least of these my brethren, you did it to me" (Matthew 25:40).

7

Marriage Issues

Dear Grace,

My brother, who is Catholic, married a non-Catholic woman. In a situation like this, does the non-Catholic have to promise to raise the children of the marriage in the Catholic faith?

The current Code of Canon Law (1983) does not require the non-Catholic to make this promise. The Code states that "the Catholic party . . . [must] promise to do all in his or her power to have all the children baptized and brought up in the Catholic Church" (canon 1125), but the non-Catholic party does not have to promise to have the children raised Catholic.

The non-Catholic party is not asked to violate his or her conscience if it requires him or her to refuse to promise to raise the children Catholic, but the Catholic party is required to do all that is possible to have the children raised in the Catholic faith. The final decision about how the children will be raised is to be a joint decision made by both parents. Canon law requires that all of this be understood by both parties before the marriage is contracted.

We know, of course, that it takes maturity and unselfishness on the part of both parents in order to raise children in a home where two religions are practiced. Children can become very confused. Great care needs to be taken when a situation like this exists. When sincere and strong love — as well as respect — exists between the parents, however, God can work miracles in that family.

These are most definitely the sorts of issues that couples contemplating marriage need to think about and discuss openly and honestly. Their future life together and the lives of their children could and probably will depend on it.

Dear Grace,

Can a Catholic who is divorced and remarried by a judge receive Communion if a priest gives him or her permission?

Under normal conditions, the answer is no. We must remember that the Holy Eucharist, or Communion, is the sacrament by which Catholics most clearly express their unity as the Body of Christ and one Church. When a person in a valid sacramental marriage contracts a civil divorce and marries another, then, by his or her actions, he or she has stepped outside the teaching of Jesus Christ and His Church that marriage is indissoluble (see Matthew 19:4-7 and Mark 10:6-9). By doing this, they have broken the bond of unity with the Church and may not receive Eucharistic Communion while the situation persists (see CCC, n. 1650).

There is such a thing as the "internal forum solution" (canon 130). There are circumstances where a priest can use the internal forum solution and allow couples in this situation to receive the sacraments under two conditions: (1) that their reception of the sacraments would not be the cause of scandal; (2) that the couple try to live according to the demands of Christian moral principles. Caution must be taken with this, however, as it has been badly abused in the past. It is an exception, not a rule.

Under this condition, those among the faithful who are divorced and remarried would not be considered to be within the situation of serious habitual sin. This is because they are persons who would not be able, for serious reasons — for example, the upbringing of the children — "to satisfy the obligation of separation" and thus assume "the task of living in full continence, that is, abstaining from the acts proper to spouses" (*Familiaris Consortio*, n. 84). On the basis of that intention, they have also received the sacrament of Penance.

It can be very difficult and painful, but most Catholics who are divorced and remarried civilly find themselves in a situation that goes directly against God's law. The problem is that many do not even know this. So, we see that for those who find that for some serious reason they cannot separate, the solution would be for them to go to Confession, receive absolution for breaking fidelity to Christ, and decide to live a life of abstinence from the sexual acts of marriage. The reason for this, of course, is because their new union is not valid in the eyes of God and His Church, since the first marriage still exists.

There are some who mistakenly see this as some kind of punishment by the Church, but the reality is that the Church is only trying to be faithful to Christ and what He taught. This is not always easy. However, there are some things that, no matter how much we wish they were different, cannot be changed because they are based on the Truth (which is God Himself), and it cannot change for anyone. God is the same — yesterday, today, and tomorrow. He is merciful, though, and knows how weak we are. At the same time, we must do all we can to understand His ways and pray that one day all Christians will come to see marriage the way Christ meant it to be — an image or reflection of the love that He had for the Church, one that is always faithful and forever.

Dear Grace,

When a person marries in a different church and gets a divorce, can he or she still marry through the Catholic Church? Is the other marriage valid?

It would be very difficult to give this question a yes or no answer without knowing more of the circumstances regarding the first marriage. Marriage cases are like puzzles with many pieces. You need all the pieces to give a correct answer. Any previous marriage ended by divorce is an impediment to another marriage, regardless of a person's religious beliefs or of the quality of the marriage. Marriages in other churches may indeed be recognized by the Catholic Church.

Catholics, as well as non-Catholics, have the right to petition the marriage tribunal to examine their marriage bond.

Canon law repeatedly stresses the permanence and indissolubility of marriage, and we believe canon law, in the case of marriage, to be based on the divine law of God. The answer of Jesus to the Pharisees in which He clearly forbids divorce and remarriage (calling the result adultery) is the basis for the canon law on the absolute indissolubility of marriage. One thing is certain: whether the first marriage was valid or invalid, it cannot be permitted for a person to contract another marriage in the Catholic Church before the nullity or the dissolution of the prior marriage has been legitimately and certainly established (see canon 1085, para. 2).

Dear Grace,

How does one handle the following situation: If you know for a fact that a couple is living together and not married, and you see them receiving Communion, do you advise the priest, or just keep quiet? Who sins more in this, the ones who are not married and receiving Communion, or the one who keeps quiet?

I am assuming that your concern stems from a sincere love and respect for the Holy Eucharist, as well as a love of neighbor. However, we must be cautious and not jump to conclusions in cases like this. For example, are you certain that you know for sure they are not married by the Church? Maybe they went to another city where they have family, or maybe a priest who lives somewhere else did the ceremony. There is also the possibility that the couple may be married legally and not be aware they are doing anything wrong. It is true, of course, that if they are not married in the Church they may not receive Holy Communion, and priests must inform them of this teaching.

According to the Code of Canon Law, "A person who is conscious of grave sin is not to receive the Body and Blood of the Lord without prior sacramental confession except for a grave reason where there is no opportunity for confession" (canon 916). Grave, or mortal, sin would be any sin whose matter is serious and which was committed freely and with knowledge of its seriousness. For sure, it would be grave matter for persons to be having sexual intercourse outside of marriage or to be in an invalid marriage. St. Paul tells us: "Whoever, therefore, eats the bread or drinks the cup of the Lord in an unworthy manner will be guilty of profaning the body and blood of the Lord. Let a man examine himself, and so eat of the bread and drink of the cup" (1 Corinthians 11:27-28).

Sometimes, even when people know they are not supposed to receive Holy Communion because of their own sinfulness, they seem to do it anyway for various reasons. They may feel embarrassed or afraid of what others will think of them if they remain seated while everyone gets up to receive the Eucharist. To answer your question, the couple receiving unworthily sins more, of course, but you also have a certain moral responsibility. If you know the couple very well in a personal way and feel that you can speak to them, then do so with care and charity. Otherwise, just speak to your pastor about the situation. He will have to handle it from that point. If you have been sincere in your heart and acted out of love to help your brother or sister in Christ, then be assured that you have done all you can, and God will honor that.

Dear Grace,

I want to have the best marriage possible, so I have begun to live with my boyfriend. We want to get to know each other really well before we get married. I know the Catholic Church is against this, but how else can we get to know each other? Why is the Church against a couple getting to know each other?

Cohabitation, which is more commonly known as "living together" in a sexual relationship outside of or before marriage, is of great concern to the Church, and it should be for everyone. It has become so widely accepted in today's society and this, in turn, has resulted in a certain blindness to the many problems and tragic unhappiness that it causes for families. You ask why the Church is against a couple getting to know each other. Unfortunately, this is a very serious misunderstanding of the Church's teaching regarding God's plan for marriage. The fact is, the very opposite is true. It is the teaching of the Church that persons contemplating marriage should get to know each other *very* well, but this is not to be done by living together without a lifelong commitment.

In his apostolic exhortation *Familiaris Consortio*, our Holy Father John Paul II tells us that every human person is called to love. This is our vocation. Everything that we know from Christian revelation shows us that the two ways that persons can truly live this vocation, or calling, are marriage and virginity. In other words, God has revealed that every person is called to one or the other: marriage or virginity. Living together has never been an option, no matter how many people are doing it.

He goes on to say that "sexuality, by means of which man and woman give themselves to one another through the acts which are proper and exclusive to spouses, is by no means something purely biological, but concerns the innermost being of the human person as such. It is realized in a truly human way only if it is an integral part of the love by which a man and a woman commit themselves totally to one another until death. The total physical self-giving would be a lie if it were not the sign and fruit of a total personal self-giving. . . . If the person were to withhold something or reserve the possibility of deciding otherwise in the future, by this very fact he or she would not be giving totally" (*Familiaris Consortio*, n. 11).

Many ask why the Church must get involved in people's personal lives. One of the most beautiful images for the Church is that of "mother." What does a mother do? She gives birth, she nurtures, she teaches, she guides. The Holy Father states that as both teacher and mother "the Church never ceases to exhort and encourage all to resolve whatever conjugal difficulties may arise without ever falsifying or compromising the truth." He adds that "to diminish in no way the saving teaching of Christ constitutes an eminent form of charity for souls" (*Familiaris Consortio*, n. 33).

How can the Church not try to protect and preserve our happiness when she knows that cohabitation increases a couple's chance of marital failure? In September of 1999, the Bishops of Pennsylvania published a document called *Living Together* in which they address some of the most common questions asked by couples today. One of them concerns this issue of "getting to know" each other. "Cohabitation is actually one of the worst ways to get to know another person, because it shortcuts the true development of lasting friendship," they write. "Those who live together before marriage often report an over-reliance on sexual expression and less emphasis on conversation and other ways of communication." Statistics show that living together reduces the possibility of a lifelong marriage, and that couples who use birth control (as those living together often do) divorce more frequently than those who do not.

In the plan of God, when we give our body to someone, we should be saying, "I give you my entire self for all my life." Things have become so upside down and far away from that plan that today those who would want to live it out in their lives are often made to feel odd or weird. The reward, however, for those who do will be great. Yes, it takes courage and much strength. We must commit ourselves to it on a daily basis if necessary. Jesus is showing us the way. All we must do is follow.

Dear Grace,

After many years of living in an abusive marriage, I happened to meet a wonderful man who showed me what real love is like. I am not in an affair with this man. We are only friends, but I know now that what I have is not a real marriage. Someone said to me once that the Catholic Church would never grant an annulment when there is a third party involved. Is that true and would it apply to me?

Your question leaves many factors missing, but there are some things we can clarify. The Catholic Church believes and teaches that the marriage bond has been established by God Himself in such a way that when it is concluded and consummated between two baptized persons, it can never be dissolved, not even by the Church (see CCC, n. 1640). In teaching this, the Church is being faithful to Jesus Christ, for it was He who stated quite clearly that marriage is indissoluble when He declared, "What therefore God has joined together, let no man put asunder" (Matthew 19:6).

What you refer to as an annulment is more properly termed a "declaration of nullity" or "decree of invalidity." This is a better way of expressing it because when we use the word "annul" it implies that we are dissolving something that really existed and that is not what the Church ever means to do. It is unfortunate that sometimes it may look or seem as if a marriage has taken place, but in actuality it may have never come into existence at all. Christian marriage is a covenant that is exchanged between a man and a woman, and when it is entered into freely and without anything to block it, then God, who is the author of marriage, seals it with His grace, and marriage comes into existence. It is for life and can never be broken.

When the Church declares a marriage null, it means that after a very careful investigation she has determined that some element or factor either prevented the marriage from coming into existence or was missing from the start. In other words, the marriage tribunal will consider what the situation was on the day of the wedding and prior to it. To all who attended the wedding, things may have looked wonderful, but underneath may have been another story.

Meeting another person years later in your marriage will have no bearing in the case, unless that was your sole reason for petitioning. Falling in love with another person can never be grounds for ending a marriage. If, however, it can be proven that your spouse had a serious psychological disorder and a history of physical abuse, which he withheld from you at the time you entered into marriage, then that would be a different matter.

Canon law allows either party to petition for a decree of nullity. Before petitioning, it is usually expected that the couple be civilly divorced. No guarantee can be given to a person who requests an investigation of their marriage that a decree of nullity will be granted. Canon law protects marriage, and all marriages are presumed to be valid and binding until death, unless proven otherwise.

Dear Grace,

May a Catholic who has had a previous marriage annulled by the Church, but whose second marriage was performed by a civil judge, rather than a priest, receive Eucharistic Communion within the laws of the Church? Or must that person first be married again within the Church before receiving Communion?

Thank you for your question, and I hope this response will clarify something that many may be wondering about. When a Catholic is granted a decree of invalidity (often referred to as an annulment), it means that a marriage was not brought about or did not come into existence on the wedding day. This does not mean that the couple did not love each other, nor does it wipe away the years they shared together. In addition, the children of the union remain legitimate in Church law. The decree of nullity does not dissolve or erase anything. What it does declare is that, for very specific reasons, a marriage did not come about. The couple is therefore free to marry in the future in the Catholic Church if they so choose.

Many mistakenly believe that a Catholic may not receive Communion if he or she is divorced. This is not true. It is being in the state of grave sin that prevents a Catholic from receiving Holy Communion. Therefore, if a Catholic enters into marriage outside of the Catholic Church, that person has broken the bonds of unity with the Church and may not, under normal conditions, have access to the reception of the sacraments of the Church (see CCC, n. 1650). So, you see, the fact that the Church declared the first "marriage" null does not change the requirement that a Catholic must marry within the Church in order to be validly and sacramentally married.

What is so unusual about the case you ask about is that this person apparently desired to do the right thing and petitioned the Church for a decree of nullity, presumably to be free to marry in the

Church, and then turned around and remarried outside the Church anyway. These situations happen, of course, sometimes even when people are trying to do their best. The law of the Church cannot change, however, for it is based on divine law. Those Catholics who contract civil unions commit adultery, in the words of Jesus (see Mark 10:11-12). Therefore, the Church maintains that such a union cannot be recognized as sacramentally valid.

Dear Grace,

I want to ask you a question. You mentioned that Communion for remarried couples who are only married by a judge is not allowable. How about couples that were once married by the Catholic Church and are now divorced and living with a person solely with the understanding that they will never marry again either by the Church or a judge? I have seen many people receiving Communion that are in this situation and I didn't think it was right.

You are correct. Persons who are living together outside of marriage are in a state of grave sin and may not receive Holy Communion. How disappointing and painful this must be for them. But we must remember that God Himself is the author of marriage. It was He who gave the first man and woman to each other in this most intimate and exclusive of unions, and He blessed it (see Genesis 1:28). Marriage is thus a communion of three persons — the husband, the wife, and God. When a couple decides to "live together," they in essence are leaving God out of the picture and this is what sin is, a turning away from God. They may not think they are doing that, but in reality they are, because they have chosen not to obey His plan for marriage.

What is tragic about this is that many couples who live together do not fully realize how wrong it is and how it offends God. His mercy, though, is greater than we could ever imagine. It may still be possible to be married by the Church through the process of convalidation, which basically means having your current marriage blessed or "sacramentalized" in the Church. Contact your pastor. Seek God's forgiveness, turn away from sin, and start over. That is the way to heaven.

Dear Grace,

If a Catholic couple is married in a civil ceremony and continues to attend Mass on a weekly basis (but not receiving Communion, of course), then divorces, how does either person once again participate in the sacrament of the Eucharist, following the divorce? An annulment would not be necessary if the original vows were not blessed by the Church, correct?

First, let us say that instead of the term "annulment," a more correct one would be "decree of invalidity." The Church cannot nullify something that never truly came into existence, and this is what is meant when the Church declares a "marriage" to be invalid.

In response to your first question, a Catholic couple married in a civil ceremony but later divorced, would each have to go to Confession before they could be allowed to receive Holy Communion again. They also could no longer be living with each other or with another person. Canon 1108 states the following: "Only those [Catholic] marriages are valid which are contracted in the presence of the local ordinary [bishop or vicar] or the pastor or priest or deacon delegated by either of them, who assist, and in the presence of two witnesses." In this case, therefore, the couple was living in an invalid marriage, one that was not recognized by the Catholic Church. Their "marriage" was not celebrated using the proper "form of marriage" — as stated in the canon quoted above. When Catholics do this, they break communion with the Mystical Body of Christ — the Church. Because this causes them to be in a state of grave sin, they are not to receive Communion while the situation persists and until they have been reconciled with God and the Church through the sacrament of Reconciliation (Confession).

With regard to your second question, a decree of invalidity for their invalid marriage is not required for them to return to the sacraments. However, if either one of this Catholic couple wishes to marry again in the Catholic Church, then a decree of invalidity would be required, even if they had not been married in the Catholic Church. There is a difference, though, between this process and the one required of a Catholic couple that married in the Church and then divorced (although both are formal cases).

In your particular situation, we would have what is known as a "lack of form" case. In order to declare the marriage invalid, it must be proven that the "form" of marriage was never present. What do we mean by this? As we have already said, canon law requires the presence of an official witness (bishop, priest, etc.) who has delegation and jurisdiction to accept the parties' consent as an official of the Church, as well as two lay witnesses who need to be present for the exchange of vows.

In the case you ask about, the couple would have to provide certain documents. First would be their baptismal certificates, showing at least one party to be a Catholic and thus demonstrating that at least one of them was bound by Catholic law to follow the proper canonical form of marriage. In addition, two civil documents are required — the marriage certificate, which verifies that the ceremony was not performed by someone authorized by the Church to assist at a wedding, and the civil divorce decree, which indicates that the civil union has been dissolved by the state.

They would also have to present some proof that their "marriage" was not celebrated in the Church before their divorce as well as proof that neither party had left the Catholic Church by a formal act before the civil wedding. In other words, since only Catholics are bound to the Catholic "form" of marriage, they must demonstrate that they were Catholic at the time of the ceremony and that this civil "marriage" did not become a sacramental marriage before their divorce. If these things can be proven, then the "lack of form" case takes only a matter of weeks to resolve.

I hope this answers your questions. Please keep in mind that there can be unusual circumstances surrounding any case. The best course of action for one or both parties to take is to speak to the pastor of their parish or the diocesan marriage tribunal. Your pastor will be happy that you want to return to the sacraments and will rejoice to have you home.

Dear Grace,

Should a man and a woman marry in the Church when they already know up front that they are physically unable to have children due to sterilization by hysterectomy in the woman?

I am assuming that by your question you are asking if the Church would consider it morally permissible for them to marry under these circumstances. The answer is yes, they may marry even if they are incapable of having children due to sterility, as long as the condition is known to both of them and has not been kept hidden in any way (see canon 1084, para. 3; see also canon 1098). The Church would have to counsel this couple very carefully, however, in order to be certain that each of them understands what they are undertaking. It would need to be explained to them that, when entering into marriage, they both completely understand and accept that no natural children will ever be born to them. This would include children brought about through any artificial means such as in vitro fertilization, artificial insemination, and surrogate motherhood. Use of these biotechnologies would be in direct opposition to the moral law of God for marriage and would therefore not be an option open to them (see *Donum Vitae*, II).

Regarding hysterectomy, we know that it is a procedure that involves removal of the uterus, thus rendering pregnancy impossible. Hysterectomy is therefore a sterilizing operation. An important question here is: What were the reasons for the hysterectomy? If the surgery was performed specifically to prevent pregnancy, then this would have been a grave sin against the human body. The woman would have to approach the Lord in the sacrament of Reconciliation, asking forgiveness for this serious offense before entering Holy Matrimony.

We know, however, that sometimes a hysterectomy is performed for therapeutic reasons when it is done to preserve the life or health of the woman. This would be morally permissible, not needing Reconciliation. The *Catechism of the Catholic Church* (n. 2297) states it this way: "Except when performed for strictly therapeutic medical reasons, directly intended *amputations*, *mutilations*, and *sterilizations* performed on innocent persons are against the moral law [cf. DS 3722]."

So, we see that a prior hysterectomy does not necessarily prevent a couple from marriage, but they would have to consider cautiously what this would mean to their future together. Perhaps your question stems from confusion between sterility and impotency. Sterility is the inability to reproduce, while impotency is the impossibility to perform the sexual acts of marriage. Impotence, unlike sterility, by its very nature invalidates marriage (see canon 1084, para. 1). This is because the sexual act is the action by which the husband and wife literally become one flesh and express their exclusive and irrevocable commitment by giving themselves totally to each other. In other words, the couple must be "capable" of consummating their marriage by sexual union, even if after marrying, they choose not to. Let us say clearly that we are not talking about what may happen later in marriage to cause impotency. As long as the marriage was capable, if you will, of being consummated in sexual union, then it is valid. Remember, marriage is for life. Once a valid marriage comes into existence, it is indissoluble (see CCC, n. 1640).

Adoption would, of course, be a wonderful possibility for this couple. There are so many unwanted innocent children in the world who are in need of a loving home and parents to care for them. This is indeed a way that a married couple can be open to life and fulfill the law of God for marriage.

8
Miscellaneous

Dear Grace,

I have not been to church in about ten years and feel that I just do not fit in, but I do so miss singing, praying, and worshipping with fellow Christians. I have always wanted to learn about Catholicism. I am a real eye sore to look at and don't want to be stared at, but I am wondering if I could find acceptance in the Catholic Church and a place to hear God's word and teaching. Can you offer any advice or direction?

It is a good thing that you have written, because I am sure there are others who may wonder the same thing. Without a doubt, you would be accepted and welcomed in the Catholic Church. This is why she is called "Catholic" — the word means "universal." She is for everybody! I can assure you that it will not matter what you look like or if you are wearing a tie, coat, or jacket. What is most important is what is in your heart.

In the Catholic Church, there is a process known as RCIA (Rite of Christian Initiation for Adults), which is specifically for persons such as you who are inquiring about entrance into the Church. You would receive instruction in the teachings and practices of the Catholic Church as well as everything it would take to become a full member.

The best thing to do first is to make an appointment to speak to the pastor of the Catholic parish closest to you. And please do not feel badly that you have not been in church in a while. Today is what counts! The priest will be so happy that you have a desire to worship God in His house and with all your other brothers and sisters in Christ. The words on his lips or in his heart will be, "Welcome home." I will be praying for you and hope that you will write again and tell me how it all worked out.

Dear Grace,

I have the following question, and I hope you can help me with the answer. Is it correct to recite the Rosary without any beads in my hand?

Yes, it is. The whole purpose of praying the Rosary is that it helps us to meditate on the life of Jesus Christ. The Lord Himself asked His disciples to pray unceasingly, so from the earliest times, His followers wanted to be faithful to His request. Thus, the custom of repetitive, meditative prayer has a long history in the life of the Church. It does happen sometimes, however, that some people place too much importance on the beads and not enough on the meditative prayer, and it is actually the meditation that is the power of the Rosary. In fact, this is how it began in the first place.

The Rosary as we know it today evolved over many centuries, but meditation on the mysteries of the life of Christ — thus, our salvation — has always been its central focus. One tradition, for example, traces the Rosary to St. Dominic de Guzman, founder of the Dominican Order. According to this account, the Blessed Virgin Mary appeared to St. Dominic and instructed him in a very unique combination of preaching and prayer that she told him would become one of the most powerful weapons against future errors and difficulties (see R. Garrigou-LaGrange, O.P., *Mother of Our Saviour and the Interior Life*, p. 293).

With time, eventually many Christians took up the practice of saying one hundred fifty Hail Marys in imitation of the monks who would recite one hundred fifty psalms contained in the Psalter or Divine Office. They believed in their hearts that Mary would always lead them to her Son, so they prayed with her and reflected on the mysteries of Jesus' life. Until recently, the full Rosary consisted of fifteen decades (or sets) of ten Hail Marys each, divided by an Our Father. Each of the decades is devoted to a major event, or "mystery," in the story of our salvation.

In October of 2002, Pope John Paul II proposed in his new apostolic letter on the Most Holy Rosary that five new mysteries be added. These are called the Luminous Mysteries (or Mysteries of Light) and it is recommended that they be prayed on Thursdays. The reason for the addition of five new mysteries is so that the Rosary may have a greater Christological depth. In other words, now we may reflect and meditate on more aspects of Jesus' life — in this case, His public ministry, that part of His life that came between His Baptism and His Passion (see *Rosarium Virginis Mariae*, n. 19). Thus, we now have a fuller story — a fuller "compendium of the Gospel."

The mysteries of the Rosary are as follows:

The Joyful Mysteries: (1) Annunciation; (2) Visitation; (3) Nativity; (4) Presentation of Christ; (5) Finding in the Temple.

The Sorrowful Mysteries: (1) Agony in the Garden; (2) Scourging; (3) Crowning with Thorns; (4) Carrying of the Cross; (5) Crucifixion.

The Glorious Mysteries: (1) Resurrection; (2) Ascension; (3) Descent of the Holy Spirit at Pentecost; (4) Assumption; (5) Coronation of the Blessed Mother.

The Luminous Mysteries: (1) Baptism of Our Lord; (2) Wedding at Cana; (3) Proclamation of the Kingdom of God; (4) Transfiguration; (5) Institution of the Eucharist.

Praying the Rosary is a spiritual exercise that is meant to draw us closer to God. The idea is not merely to have a rule or a count of how many prayers we recite. Holding the beads in your hands is good, but the most important part is the prayer and reflection. Our Holy Father calls the Rosary "a training in holiness" (*Rosarium Virginis Mariae*, n. 5) in that it commits the faithful to contemplate the Christian mystery. This is the key and secret to the power of the Rosary — it is a beautiful method of contemplation that leads us closer to Christ, and this in turn will lead us to desire to become more like Him.

Dear Grace,

If we were to miss Sunday Mass, would it suffice to recite the Rosary to compensate?

It depends on the reason for missing Mass. If the reason was intentional, then that would constitute a mortal sin and could not be made up by reciting the Rosary. If, however, you missed Mass and had good reason (illness, caring for others, unable to get to a Church, etc.), then reciting the Rosary, or meditating on Scripture on that day, or going to Mass on another day of that week would be acceptable and good.

Dear Grace,

I would appreciate it if you would clarify the position of the Catholic Church regarding Freemasonry. Is it compatible with our faith?

Freemasonry, which dates from the year 1717, is not considered to be compatible with the Catholic faith. Because it was a secret society that had shown itself to be radically anti-Catholic, Pope Clement XII, in 1738, issued a solemn and definitive condemnation of Freemasonry and everything related to it, absolutely prohibiting Catholics from becoming members. The Church has repeated this teaching in at least three hundred other documents, statements, and solemn pronouncements.

Freemasonry is organized very much like a religion in that it "displays all the elements of religion, and as such it becomes a rival to the religion of the Gospel. It includes temples and altars, prayers, a moral code, worship, vestments, feast days, the promise of reward and punishment in the afterlife, a hierarchy, and initiative and burial rites" (*The New Catholic Encyclopedia*, vol. 6, p. 137). The differences between its teaching and those of the Catholic Church are numerous.

The pope who most strongly spoke out against Freemasonry was Leo XIII, in his 1884 encyclical *Humanum Genus* (On

Freemasonry). Pope Leo was concerned that although the Freemasons make many things public, "there are many things like mysteries which it is the fixed rule to hide with extreme care, not only from strangers, but also from their very many members, such as their secret and final designs, the names of the chief leaders, and certain secret and inner meetings, as well as their decisions, and the ways and means of carrying them out" (n. 9). In other words, much is hidden from their very own members. It is conceivable, then, that some members may not be aware that their beliefs are contrary to the Catholic faith.

The Church has imposed the penalty of excommunication on Catholics who become Freemasons. The penalty of excommunication for joining the Masonic Lodge was explicit in the 1917 Code of Canon Law (canon 2335), and it is implicit in the 1983 edition (canon 1374). Because the revised and current Code of Canon Law is not explicit on this point, some thought mistakenly that the Church's prohibition of Freemasonry had changed. As a result of this confusion, shortly before the 1983 code was promulgated, the Congregation for the Doctrine of the Faith issued a statement indicating that the penalty was still in force.

The following is part of the most recent decree from the Vatican on the subject of Freemasonry, issued on November 26, 1983: "The Church's negative judgment in regard to Masonic associations remains unchanged, since their principles have always been considered irreconcilable with the doctrine of the Church and therefore membership in them remains forbidden. The faithful who enroll in Masonic associations are in a state of grave sin and may not receive Holy Communion."

Let us keep in mind, of course, that God loves every human person, even those who are separated from Him and His Church. Every individual is called to conversion and repentance. It is up to all of us to pray for one another's salvation. Love is ultimately the answer to all division and disunity.

Dear Grace,

Someone said to me that Our Lady of Guadalupe is not the Blessed Virgin Mary. Is this true?

I can only imagine how surprised you were at hearing that, but rest assured, it is not true. Since the third century, there have been reported an uncounted number of appearances of the Mother of God — although not all have been recognized as authentic — and they have all been the same beautiful lady. In order to distinguish one apparition from another, however, Mary will almost always be referred to with a title that indicates the place where she appeared or some other significant aspect of the appearance.

Among some of the most famous apparitions that have been recognized by the Church are the following:

1531 — Our Lady of Guadalupe, Guadalupe, Mexico: On a hill outside Mexico City, the Blessed Mother appeared four times to a recent convert to Christianity, Juan Diego. Mary proclaimed herself "the Mother of the true God who gives life," and left her image permanently upon St. Juan Diego's tilma, or mantle.

1830 — Our Lady of the Miraculous Medal, Paris, France: In the chapel of the Daughters of Charity of St. Vincent de Paul, Mary showed herself three times to novice Catherine Labouré (age twenty-four), who said she was commissioned by the Virgin to have the medal of the Immaculate Conception or "Miraculous Medal" made in order to spread devotion to our Lady.

1858 — Our Lady of Lourdes, Lourdes, France: At the Grotto of Massabielle, the Virgin showed herself eighteen times to Bernadette Soubirous (age fourteen). Under the title "the Immaculate Conception," she called for penance and prayer for the conversion of sinners.

1917 — Our Lady of Fátima, Fátima, Portugal: While tending sheep, Lucia de Santos (age ten) and her two cousins, Francisco (age nine) and Jacinta Marto (age seven), reported six apparitions of Mary, who identified herself as "Our Lady of the Rosary." Mary urged prayer of the Rosary, penance for the conversion of sinners, and consecration of Russia to her Immaculate Heart.

One may wonder why Mary is so persistent. Why has she come so many times and why does she keep coming back? Obviously, she has an urgent message to convey. Our Holy Father John Paul II beautifully explains for us, in his encyclical letter *Redemptoris Mater* ("Mother of the Redeemer"), that she who was chosen by God to be Mother of the Redeemer is also the mother of all mankind "in the order of grace." As a mother, therefore, she joins us in our pilgrimage toward our heavenly destiny. Would any good mother ever forget her children, ever leave them abandoned? It is easy to imagine that in heaven she must plead with her Son to send her "one more time" to help her children find their way to Him. Every appearance she makes is for the ultimate purpose of turning us back to God. She loves us so much. How can we not listen to her? Jesus did.

The local bishop is the first and main authority in apparition cases, which can be defined as instances of private revelation. Bishops evaluate evidence of an apparition according to very strict guidelines. If the bishop recognizes a Marian apparition, it means that the message is not contrary to faith and morals, and that Mary may be venerated in a special way at the site. But, because the Church does not require belief in a private revelation, Catholics are free to decide how much personal spiritual emphasis to place on apparitions and the messages they deliver. We should always remain open, however, to something that has been recognized as authentic by the Church.

About the Author

✤

Grace MacKinnon, a syndicated columnist, writer, public speaker, and teacher, has taken on the mission of helping adult Catholics and non-Catholics come to a better knowledge and understanding of the beauty and richness of the truth found in the Catholic faith. Ms. MacKinnon holds a Master of Arts degree in theology and is an instructor in Catholic doctrine for adults for the Catholic Diocese of Brownsville. She teaches courses on a variety of Catholic topics in the Lower Rio Grande Valley of south Texas and is a welcomed speaker at conferences, meetings, and workshops throughout the U.S. Her teaching CDs and audiotapes are available through St. Joseph Communications at www.saintjoe.com or by calling 1-800-526-2151.

Ms. MacKinnon's syndicated newspaper column, "Dear Grace," has been in publication since August 1999 in both Catholic and secular publications. Welcoming readers' questions and carefully answering them in accordance with Church teachings, she relies on Scripture, papal encyclicals, canon law, the writings of the Church Fathers and other orthodox sources, and in particular on the *Catechism of the Catholic Church*.

For more information on the author and her column, please visit www.DearGrace.com or write to her at Grace@DearGrace.com.

Index

186 _"Dear Grace"_

Hail Mary, 63-64
Handbook of Indulgences, 36, 46
Heaven, 15-16, 18, 20-21, 23-24, 26, 28, 30-33, 36, 49-51, 55-56, 58, 62-63, 67-68, 73-74, 76, 79-81, 84-87, 90-91, 111, 118-119, 123, 126-128, 150, 170, 180
Helena, St., 45
Hell, 23-24, 29-33, 35, 55, 79, 84, 86, 141-142
Heresy, 34
Hildebrand, Alice von, 9-10
Hippo, Council of, 20, 59
Holy Days of Obligation, 122, 128, 148
Holy Door of the Holy Year of Jubilee, 46-48
Holy Land, 45
Holy Orders (see Priests; Deacons)
Holy Saturday, 111
Holy Week, 86, 110-111
Homoousios, 39
Horn of a Ram, 46
Host, Communion, 75, 97-98, 102-103, 114, 120
House of Prayer, 119
Humanum Genus (On Free-masonry), 177
Hypostatic Union, 39, 90
Hysterectomy, 172-173

Ignatius of Antioch, St., 50-51, 58, 79
In Persona Christi, 68, 74
In Vitro Fertilization, 172
Incarnation, The, 25, 27, 39, 94

Incarnationis Mysterium (On the Great Jubilee of the Year 2000), 48
Indissolubility of Marriage, 163
Indulgence, 35-36, 46
Infallibility, 27-29
Infertility, 136
Innocent XI, Pope, 45
Intercessory Prayer, 15
Intinction (see also Communion, Holy; Eucharist), 97
Invalidity, Decree of, 167-168, 170-171
Iraq, 61
Isaiah, 52

Jacinta Marto, Blessed, 9, 179
Jansenism, 86-87
Jeremiah, 92
Jerome, St., 45
Jesus Christ Superstar, 59
Jesus Christ, 11, 15-17, 19-24, 25-31, 33, 36-40, 43-46, 48-65, 67-70, 72-79, 81-85, 87-90, 92, 94, 96-98, 104-114, 116-117, 119-123, 126-128, 131-136, 141-145, 151, 154, 156-157, 161, 163, 166-167, 169, 175-176, 180
    as Mediator, 15
    as Messiah, 28, 38, 52
    as Son of God, 25, 28, 30-31, 38-40, 52
John Paul II, Pope, 22, 42, 48, 54, 92-93, 132, 134, 138, 143, 151, 159, 165, 176, 180

FATHER PETER STRAVINSKAS HAS *THE CATHOLIC ANSWER* FOR YOU!

Since 1987, inquiring Catholic minds have turned to Our Sunday Visitor's bimonthly magazine *The Catholic Answer*, edited by Father Stravinskas, for the answers to such questions as:

- Can anyone other than a Catholic ever receive Holy Communion in a Catholic Church? (Book 1)
- If a Catholic still has guilty feelings about past sins, what should he do? (Book 2)
- Why did the Lord God give Satan the power to do with Job as he willed? (Book 3)

Now you, too, can discover the solid Catholic answers to these and many other questions gleaned from the pages of this award-winning magazine and compiled in a handy book format.

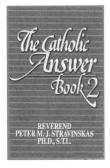

The Catholic Answer Book, 0-87973-458-2, **(458)** paper, 192 pp.

The Catholic Answer Book 2, 0-87973-737-9, **(737)** paper, 240 pp.

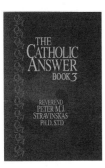

The Catholic Answer Book 3, 0-87973-933-9, **(933)** paper, 304 pp.

Our Sunday Visitor

200 Noll Plaza, Huntington, IN 46750
Toll Free: **1-800-348-2440**
E-mail: osvbooks@osv.com
Website: www.osv.com

Our Sunday Visitor . . .
Your Source for Discovering the Riches of the Catholic Faith

Our Sunday Visitor has an extensive line of materials for young children, teens, and adults. Our books, Bibles, booklets, CD-ROMs, audios, and videos are available in bookstores worldwide.

To receive a FREE full-line catalog or for more information, call **Our Sunday Visitor** at **1-800-348-2440**. Or write, **Our Sunday Visitor** / 200 Noll Plaza / Huntington, IN 46750.

- -

Please send me: __A catalog
Please send me materials on:
__Apologetics and catechetics   __Reference works
__Prayer books   __Heritage and the saints
__The family   __The parish
Name_____
Address_____Apt._____
City_____State_____Zip_____
Telephone (   ) _____

A33BBABP

- -

Please send a friend: __A catalog
Please send a friend materials on:
__Apologetics and catechetics   :__Reference works
__Prayer books   __Heritage and the saints
__The family   __The parish
Name_____
Address_____Apt._____
City_____State_____Zip_____
Telephone (   ) _____

A33BBABP

- -

OurSundayVisitor

200 Noll Plaza, Huntington, IN 46750
Toll Free: **1-800-348-2440**
E-mail: osvbooks@osv.com
Website: www.osv.com